OH MY GOODNESS!

GROW YOUR VIRTUES
AND FLOURISH

SHIREEN CHADA

Oh My Goodness!
Grow Your Virtues and Flourish
Shireen Chada

Published by Release Your Wings (www.releaseyourwings.net),
a Brahma Kumaris/USA (www.brahmakumaris.org/us) production.

Quotes without attribution are original to the author.

ISBN 13 Paperback: 978-1-941883-06-8
ISBN 13 Ebook: 978-1-941883-05-1
ISBN 13 Audiobook: 978-1-941883-07-5

Cover and book design by Judi Rich
Cover image by Bebe Butler

For worldwide distribution.

DEDICATED TO

To

Dadi Janki *(1916-present)*
Among all the people I've met in this life, you
most embody the virtues I describe herein.

And

Bebe Butler (1974-2016)
You taught me invaluable lessons of how to
embrace virtues even in the most difficult of
circumstances. You were a master in the art
of composing meditations. Whatever value
or skill may be found in the meditations in
this book owe a great debt to you.

TABLE OF CONTENTS

INTRODUCTION

This book is for you if, and only if, you think your life could be at least a little better, happier, more peaceful, and more meaningful. This book is also for you if on your way to personal happiness and meaning, you want to help make the world a better place for everyone.

Most people would agree that today's world, in various ways, is seriously off course. To right its course, the world needs nothing less than a renaissance of virtue, a reemphasizing of personal goodness. How can we empower our own virtue, so that we achieve a joyful life and play our role in restoring the world? Let this book, *Oh My Goodness!* be your friend and guide on that journey.

In the past few decades, some bestselling books have told us to just focus on our selfish goals, visualize our material desires, and our thoughts will magnetically attract our objectives. This is not one of those books! Why not? Because, first we must clearly and reasonably grasp what is truly good for us, what will make us profoundly happy and fulfilled. In other words, we must be sure we have the right aims.

Psychology shows that we are often bad at forecasting what will make us happy. We choose the wrong goals, and even if we achieve them, we are not happy. Nor does the world become a better place for all our self-serving schemes.

This book does not encourage magical unearned empowerment. Rather, I try to show you a simple way to find and earn real, lasting joy. And that which we earn, we can keep. The universe is structured that way. It is through virtue, goodness, that we earn permanent joy and wisdom.

As the **Beatles** so eloquently said it, "Money can't buy me love." Nor can material power, vanity, or lust buy us love. This book gives you practical remedies to heal the soul and make tangible life progress. Anyone that claims you can be happy without virtue is telling you a tall tale. The path to real happiness requires us to embrace and cultivate our inherent goodness.

Our virtues are a source of perpetual happiness for the soul. We learn this from millennia of human wisdom, voluminous social science, and our own life experience. Happiness comes from the true self -- and our true self is rich in goodness. Hence, the path to happiness is the path to self-realization. By connecting to our real self, the seat of all virtue, we experience a spiritual happiness that no amount of material toys can ever give us.

Who you really are is precisely what the world needs. If you want perfect happiness, just BE YOURSELF! Your true self. The more you cultivate virtue, the more you discover yourself.

Here are some insights from our wise friends who lived in different times and places, yet expressed in universal terms our need to return to our core virtues.

"With virtue and quietness, one may conquer the world."
— Lao Tzu

"Virtue does not come from wealth, but wealth and every other good thing that men have comes from virtue.
— Socrates

"Till I have your disposition, your goodness,
I never can have your happiness."
— Jane Austen, *Pride and Prejudice.*
(Lizzie is talking to her sister Jane.)

As Austen's Elizabeth Bennet suggested, to bring joy into our lives, we must cultivate goodness, which manifests as practical virtues. We should seek virtue not just as a moral rule but, because of virtue's intrinsic value, as virtue justifies itself as we shall see in this book.

I guarantee that when you reflect on the virtues and do the meditations presented in this book, you will see your life rapidly improving. The process is simple, but not necessarily easy. Real self-transformation never is. It requires a lot of honesty and spiritual effort. But the reward more than repays the effort. I invite you to plant the seeds of virtue in your mind, water them with constant reflection, and let them blossom in your heart. You will flourish.

And by the way, what are the virtues? Read on!

Special Note: I've included in this book ten meditations from a very dear friend Bebe Butler (1974 - 2016). Bebe was an exceptional spiritual practitioner. She was also one of the most artistically creative people I have ever known. Bebe had a special gift for creating meditations. One could say that creative meditations are Bebe's signature legacy.

Bebe so much deserves to be remembered, and to help that happen, I've included her meditations in this book. Her meditations survive in the audio form, and we transcribed them for this book. Her audio meditations are available on YouTube (http://www.youtube.com/releaseyourwings) and will also be available to download along with the audio meditations of this book.

HOW TO USE THIS BOOK?

To cultivate virtues is entirely in our self-interest because of the intimate link between virtues and real happiness. To bring virtues powerfully into your life, you must do two things:

1. Practice reflecting on them
2. At least once a day, implement a virtue in your life.

This book, *Oh My Goodness!* will enable you to do this. This book will fully and clearly explain how you can easily cultivate virtues. I will provide you with the tools. After that, you must step forward for your own happiness. To achieve the joyful and meaningful life you desire, you must practice, practice, practice!

"And you? When will you begin that long journey into yourself?"
— Rumi

Here's the deal: As you go through your day, accentuate a virtue by reflecting on it. Then look a little deeper into your innate, core goodness, and engage it at least once a day. This will help you still your mind and pay your bills (just kidding about the stilling your mind bit!).

I'll unwrap thirty-nine virtues in this book. Based on many years of experience, I'll rate each one of them in one of three categories: 1. Beginner; 2. Intermediate; 3. Advanced. Within these categories, the virtues are not prioritized. They are given in simple alphabetical order. For example, in the beginner category, "appreciation" is not more important, nor easier, than "beauty."

Don't demand too much of yourself too soon, because you will lose your enthusiasm. Take it slow and steady. Whether you are taking a yoga class, a golf class, or algebra, they all have beginner, intermediate, and advanced levels. This is true for everything on earth that is worth learning. If you give advanced math to a math beginner, you will confuse and discourage that person. This is so true for the virtues. So, go at your own pace and read through the book. If you have difficulty with one of the easy or intermediate virtues, just do the best you can. You can always come back later and work on it. Start reflecting on each virtue and practice them by doing the meditations. Even at the beginner level, as you begin to advance in one virtue, you will strengthen the other virtues. Every virtue you cultivate nourishes the others.

One of the best things about virtues is that just by reflecting on them, they start to blossom inside you. Take a virtue, reflect on it, and do the meditation associated with it. Give yourself time with each virtue – that may be a day or even a week.

Go through the virtues one at a time from beginner to advanced level. And once you have finished the book, you can use it in a special way to deal with special situations or heavy decisions. Open the book to any page, pick the virtue listed on that page, and tell yourself, "This is the virtue I need today." The universe of virtues works in magical ways. I've noticed that the virtue you will need that day will appear to you. You will give your day an added resource to make it truly successful and enjoyable. You should also use this book in that same way when you are embarking on an important new project. Again, open the book to a random page and make that virtue your north star to guide that project or situation.

Special note: The book includes 39 downloadable audio meditations. These meditations bring the virtues to life and empower you to be your best self. Listen carefully to these meditations daily and see the change in your life.

For goodness sake, let's go on a journey...

Refer to page 70 for the link to free audios of all the meditations featured in this book.

BEGINNER VIRTUES

APPRECIATION

When we study an important book, we often highlight key passages. In the same way, we need a spiritual highlighter for our lives. As we go through life, appreciation is a way to consciously mark moments and insights that have profound meaning for us, so we don't forget them.

Appreciation is to walk through life with this highlighter, intentionally looking for those moments or scenes, events or persons that are worth cherishing and remembering. When you carry a spiritual highlighter, you create the habit of noticing, focusing, and amplifying goodness. This is an amazing way to increase your joy. So pick up your spiritual highlighter and begin a simple exercise of noticing the most worthy aspects of people and things around you.

Appreciation is essential for our spiritual progress. Because, if we don't appreciate things, they slip away from us. Everyone in this world has up moments and down moments, but those who go through life with appreciation enjoy an abundant life.

Riches don't just come from accumulating grown-up toys. Riches come from perceiving things in the right way, with appreciation. This practice also creates a wave of joy and sunshine in your life. Nowadays, it seems natural to emphasize what's wrong in life, because of the prevailing mood around us.

However, these conscious exercises are essential to protect us from unhappy but powerful subconscious feelings. If you don't build these conscious exercises into your life, your negative subconscious patterns will control your life and leave you unhappy.

MEDITATION ON
APPRECIATION

Sit comfortably where you can be still for a few moments. Take a deep breath and while releasing this breath, relax your legs. You're relaxed. Take another deep breath and release this breath and relax your stomach area. You're even more relaxed. Take another deep breath and release this breath slowly and relax your shoulders and arms. You're totally relaxed.

In this state of relaxation, you are connected to your core being, to the real you... Now, take a few moments and reflect on your life. Reflect on all the things that are profound, nourishing, and good in your life. Take a mental highlighter and highlight these aspects one at a time. If you are having a difficult time finding something to highlight, then just take a few more moments and think of one valuable thing in your life. It could be your work, it could be your faith, it could be your family, it could be your friends, or it could be a very inspiring moment you had even 10 years or more in the past. Consciously highlight this situation or person. And say to yourself, "This is worthy of my appreciation."

Be intentional and again look for moments or scenes or persons that are worth appreciating. If you are not able to do it, take a break and come back to this meditation later.

Now tell yourself, "This will be my practice from now on. I will carry a spiritual highlighter with me and notice the best aspects of events, situations, and people around me."

After a few days of this practice, you begin to notice the amazing way appreciation is increasing your joy. You begin to discover more and more things that are worthy of appreciation in your life. You start to notice how rich and full of sunshine your life really is.

Om Shanti—I am Peace.

Refer to page 70 for the link to free audios of all the meditations featured in this book.

BEAUTY

If you really think about it, there is something amazing about our very existence. Look closely, and you will find beauty everywhere. There is beauty in a grain of sand, in a snowflake, in a water crystal, and in the galaxies above us. And, we find beauty in the living, conscious self, myself, and in others.

Next time you take a walk, stop and look very closely at a leaf or tree or the sky. If you look closely enough, you will see the wondrous beauty in nature. We inhabit a universe of art, whether the art of a waterfall or a leaf.

Beauty is not only visual. We discover beautiful sounds, scents, and savor beautiful flavors. We meet beautiful people, and experience beautiful moments.

To embrace spiritual beauty is to deeply experience the aesthetics of moments and qualities in our daily lives. It is to observe what is lovely and good around us. It means taking out our spiritual camera, putting on our sacred lens and taking snapshots of exquisite moments in our life. This lens lets us see the blessings we constantly receive in our day-to-day life.

To cultivate beauty in my life, I must become a spiritual photographer and capture moments of grace. As the saying goes, beauty is in the eye of the beholder. Only by learning to take my spiritual camera around do I realize that I am actually witnessing beauty. We discover our link to beauty only when we fasten the lens and begin to notice and take snapshots of life itself. Then we behold what an amazing magnificent world we live in. Beauty is catching a glimpse of nature's genius, or watching a moving exchange between two souls and thinking, that is glorious! It has enriched my life.

Seasoned artistic photographers work with something called "photography prompts." For example, a prompt could be a phrase such as, "outdoor concert" or even "sliced watermelon." These prompts, either a word or a phrase, inspire a photograph. The phrase is typically used as a theme and gives the artist purpose and direction. Photography prompts help the artist to look at even the most mundane subject in unique ways and enhance the "photographic eye."

In the same way, to notice spiritual beauty in our lives we can use "sacred photography prompts" and develop our "inner photographic eye." We can train ourselves to be more observant and find beauty even in the most apparently mundane scenes. We can inspire our daily beauty shots by picking a theme each day such as well-being, freedom, generosity, coolness, learning, and tranquility to name a few. So, let's say we pick "hope" as a theme for a particular day. We can then be alert to beautiful scenes of hope and capture them as a beauty shot. I've noticed that once we have a prompt, we will find ample beautiful "photo opportunities" to fit that theme.

So, my dear friends, let's take around our spiritual camera and develop our inner photographic eye. Remember, beauty is in the eye of the beholder. So may you behold nothing but transcendent beauty.

MEDITATION ON
BEAUTY

To cultivate beauty, I must become a spiritual photographer and capture moments of grace in my life. As the saying goes, beauty is in the eye of the beholder. Let's work with spiritual "photography prompts" in this meditation to capture beautiful moments in my life. These prompts, usually a virtue, will give our spiritual photographs purpose and direction.

Imagine a still mountain lake in the morning. Notice the serenity and beauty of that mountain lake and allow it to permeate your being as you breathe it in and become as still as its waters. Let yourself soak in this stillness for a few moments and savor the peace you are feeling.

You are feeling as still and calm as the mountain lake. In this state of stillness, pick your word prompt for the day. Pick something that will inspire you, a value that you hold dear. Let's say your theme for the day is kindness.

Now, take out your spiritual camera and think of at least one moment of kindness you witnessed or offered to someone. Take a few moments, go back to your still center, and now again think of your beauty shot of kindness. Remember, to begin with, we just need to reflect on one interaction. Continue to reflect on this interaction. Continue to take snapshots of this interaction from all angles.

After some practice, you begin to sense the beauty of kindness all around you. You notice little things that seem so ordinary but were beautiful acts of kindness. You begin to feel the beauty, the peace as it unfolds in your day-to-day interactions.

Now, take some time to remember that you are spirit. You are innately beautiful, and you have the power to see beauty. The only reason you lost touch with beauty is because you forgot your inner lens. You are light, you are eternal, and you are lovely.

Om Shanti – I am Peace.

CONTENTMENT

Feeling sustained and being content are deeply connected. Sustenance comes from three sources. One, our steadfast commitment to remaining satisfied no matter what the circumstances. This sustains our mind and heart.

Two, spending quality time with the Source strengthens our understanding of where real-life sustenance comes from.

Three, we find sustenance when we first embrace being and then proceed to doing, instead of leaping into this world of doing and competition and images.

Let us first create spiritual space for ourselves and find sustenance and fulfillment through being in our relationship to the Source. In this space, you no longer run madly around, chasing, competing, comparing...

When you deny space in your head to comparison, competition, criticism, and complaints, then contentment happens. We must remove the above four deadly "C" words to attain true satisfaction. We indulge in the four deadly "Cs" out of arrogance. For example, we criticize because we think we are better than others. This is subtle arrogance because we think we know the real story when we probably don't.

In contrast to the four unhealthy 'Cs,' knowing that a Higher Power loves me contributes directly to my contentment. This may sound trite precisely because it's so true. We develop strength and contentment by learning the Source's way of loving. This gives us courage to accept who we are; and the way that we are. When we truly experience this love that can only come from a higher Source, then this love fulfills us so much that we experience deep contentment, security, and the certainty that we will be taken care of. Someone much stronger than us is always here with us. Then we have no need or urge to chase unnecessary things. We have the strength to easily drop the four "Cs."

MEDITATION ON
CONTENTMENT

by Bebe Butler (1974 – 2016)

Much of the time we try to satisfy the appetite of the soul with the things of the world. We fill ourselves with relationships, and we satisfy the cravings of our desires. We fill ourselves with position and external things of the world but in the same way empty calories leave you unsatisfied; we find that the soul still feels an emptiness inside. It still feels a craving, a hunger for something deeper.

Contentment merely means that the belly of the soul is full. It wants nothing because it feels so satisfied with the real substance of the soul.

Take a deep breath now and leave your world. Move to the edge of the world where there is nothing physical. No sound, no drama, no responsibilities to uphold, just let them all go. As you settle into a place of silence and stillness, in front of you is a radiant sunlight of spiritual energy full of all the beautiful things of the self, love, light, peace. Allow yourself to fill with this light. Let the rays of peace and serenity enter into you and breathe them in fully. Fill the belly of the soul with the vibrations of pure, peaceful spiritual energy.

With each breath, you savor and take in even more peace. And, knowing that love is what the universe is made of, breathe in that energy of gentleness radiating from this light, that energy of love, connection, belonging, and feel yourself connected to the whole of humanity— breathing as one as we take in the energy of pure spiritual love.

Notice how light you begin to feel, how weightless, as if there is no gravity and allow yourself to soak and bathe and take in the energy of pure joy. What does it feel like to completely fill the belly of the soul with the energy of joy and see this light pouring into you and creating a warm inner smile in your heart?

If I want to experience contentment and satisfaction, every now and then I have to learn to step away from the world and move into silence and stillness. I need to take a vacation away from the world so I can go and fill the belly of the soul with real eternal, imperishable beautiful qualities of the spirit that give me a feeling of fullness, complete satisfaction, and a quiet joy that makes me feel as if all is well in my world and it is only getting better.

Om Shanti – I am Peace.

CREATIVITY

Our best works of art or creative expressions come when we are so silent that a higher Power creates through us. Even many of the greatest artists expressed this sentiment. You are receiving creative inspiration, rather than manufacturing it all on your own.

Creativity happens in humility and silence. In this sublime space, we open up and accept creative inspiration. This can be in the form of creating spiritual exercises for yourself, or looking at things in a new way, or refreshing your daily routine with new insights. Creativity flows through us best when we are in silence, connected to the Source, and we allow the Source to work through us.

The true artist is never alone, and that's what brings humility. I'm not just talking about physical works of art but also thoughts and consciousness. At least once a day, it is good to sit down and say to yourself, I want to create a beautiful thought. Then become still, receive inspiration from God and create that beautiful thought. This helps us to avoid getting stuck in the daily grind. It brings freshness to our lives. It brings newness, takes us out of our comfort zone, and makes life exciting.

Creativity is also allowing the Source to work on you and create a new you. After all, He/She is the ultimate artist, right? You can not only create newness, but you can receive newness as a gift. The highest form of creativity is to allow yourself to become a new you. In this aspect of creativity, you are creating and receiving new thoughts at every moment not just recycling the same old thought patterns.

Do something small but new and unusual every day, something that gets you out of your rut and routine. While doing simple tasks, ask yourself, "What can I do differently to break my habit of being stuck in this rut?" Whether it's a dance with God or a walk in nature in the evening or taking your meditation outside and looking up at the sky and practicing silence, this new approach allows creative inspiration to come through.

Creativity is a colorful energy. It's fresh and inspiring, it feels new, it has a charge. The enemy of creativity is too much busy-ness. When I just go, go, go, I lose my inspiration. Silence renews and recharges creativity, whereas if we stay so busy, busy, busy and distracted, that new fresh energy isn't there. When I start to nurture my soul even a little bit, I will be inspired. Creativity innovates.

MEDITATION ON
CREATIVITY

Creativity best flows through us when we are in silence and connected to the Source. When we allow the Source to work through us, then we receive creative inspiration instead of manufacturing it all on our own. For this, we must learn to be silent and open.

Just for a few moments, let's leave the world of work, roles, and responsibilities far behind. Let's visualize a beautiful, clear blue sky above us. Look at the sky and see how open and quiet it is up there. Take a deep breath and breathe in the peace. Take another deep breath and feel a gentle breeze on your face. Your mind is beginning to feel as clear as the sky. Rest in this space for a few moments.

From this space of harmony, you invite the Source to work on you and through you. You also allow yourself to create a new thought in this moment. Talk to yourself, "I am light. I am love. I am a luminous being of sweetness and humility. I invite the Source to work on me and create a new me." Light from the Source is cascading over you. You feel so still inside. You are in touch with what is most valuable and creative inside yourself.

Continue to absorb this soothing, light energy into yourself. You feel so fresh and inspired. For a few more moments you stay in the silence. This silence renews and recharges your creativity.

Om Shanti – I am Peace.

ENCOURAGEMENT

To encourage is to shine a light on someone's heart, on their core good qualities. It is to help others deploy those qualities to navigate life. How can we genuinely encourage people? We must first find their motivation point and give them strength to follow through. Everyone has goodness and positive values within them. We have to find and shine a light on them. When we do it well, people get up and progress in life. Encouragement heartens people to move forward. It helps them do their best.

Discouragement is the opposite of determination. Discouraged people have lost their determination. They've lost their courage. We encourage them by reminding them again and again of their innate goodness, their inner determination and courage. We can do that if we really understand people and remind them of what's inside them. Even though encouragement seems to imply that we tell others to do something, the best encouragement is to show them what's inside of them. We inspire ourselves to live in love, to motivate others to live in their own dignity and determination.

MEDITATION ON
ENCOURAGEMENT

Encouragement means that I remind others of what is good and pure in them again and again and again. This happens when I remind them of what is really inside them. Not, what they think is inside them, but to help them discover that their core, their innate nature, is peace, love, and light.

Visualize yourself sitting on a beautiful mountain. You can feel the fresh, clean breeze on your face. There is a waterfall next to you; you can hear the pristine water cascade down the mountain. It is so tranquil here. Breathe this stillness deeply into yourself. Take another deep breath of this fresh mountain air and this silence and let it permeate every fiber of your being. You feel completely relaxed and light.

Now pour this stillness and love and light onto the world. Imagine that you are filling your mind with silence, and on rays of spiritual light, you are letting this cascade onto the people you know, and onto the people in the world. Now fill your mind with love. Go deep within and access your loving goodness, and again on the rays of spiritual light send this to the world. Access your wisdom and pour it onto the world like a waterfall. It is washing away the worries of the world and the discouragement. It is cleaning every mind and refreshing every heart. Keep visualizing this wise light as it cascades over the entire world, encouraging hearts.

Om Shanti – I am Peace.

ENTHUSIASM

The original meaning of the word enthusiasm is very apt for its current meaning. The word is derived from Greek meaning, "to be inspired or possessed by a god, to be rapt, to be in ecstasy."

Enthusiasm happens when you surrender your energy to God, or in other words, all your eggs are in one basket and your energy is connected to God and filled with God. Even the talents that God wants to use in your life are infused with this Divine energy. Yes, you have excitement, you have inspiration, you have ideas, and you want to use them, but you are working with God's energy instead of your own. You are working with God's ideas instead of your own. It's a quality that comes from surrendering your energies to that connection. Then you are filled with that divine spirit. This kind of divine enthusiasm uplifts the soul.

Before we can experience enthusiasm, we must have interest -- an interest in life, interest in people, and interest in voluntary service. I had an aunt who had no formal education, never went to school (not even first grade), yet she had so much zest for life. She had a really hard life, but never gave that as an excuse for not being curious about the people around her, nor to find time to do what she liked (cooking). We all loved being around her because her enthusiasm for life was so infectious. I feel that her enthusiasm came from following her interest.

This is what makes us lively and makes life worth living. Yes, the daily routine of life is important. It is necessary to do certain things every day. However, to keep our enthusiasm for life, we must find things that truly interest us, and then devote some part of the day to doing those things.

The opposite of enthusiasm is laziness. When we are lazy, we don't bother to learn about people, or discover and pursue our interests, nor even learn about the country we are living in. Both busy-ness and laziness prevent you from accessing your enthusiasm.

MEDITATION ON
ENTHUSIASM

The word enthusiasm is derived from ancient Greek language meaning "filled with the spirit of God." True enthusiasm comes when we commit our energy to the Source and when we live in our real self.

The opposite of enthusiasm is a laziness of spirit. We may be busy with tasks and worries and what people said and what people did, but our mind is trapped in the same old thought patterns. And, when our mind is stuck, then there is a lack of real interest.

To move away from this lack of motivation and go toward enthusiasm, we must learn to work from the divine energy of the Source.

See yourself sitting and watching a beautiful sunset over the ocean. You are taking in the golden orange rays of the sun kissing the ocean waves. As you are watching the waves, imagine all your scenes and situations washing away from your mind.

Now, envision the golden light of the Source coming toward you from the Sun. Rays of light and love and acceptance are washing over you. You sense that this is the purest highest energy. You deeply know that the Source will always be there for you and never misuse your trust. Allow yourself in this moment to be connected to the Divine's light. This light is filling every part of your mind. In this space, you say to yourself, "I surrender my energy to this Source. I surrender my talents and ideas." You begin to feel infused with a different kind of energy - an excitement that is pure and clean.

With this simple practice of connecting and receiving energy from the Source, you learn to just be in peace. You discover your zest for life, your passions, and your joys. This renews your life and you move to a place of enthusiasm.

Om Shanti – I am Peace.

INTROSPECTION

Introspection, "looking inward," is an easy virtue to practice, easier than, say, forgiveness. We have to understand the importance of turning our attention inwards, away from the external side life. Normally we focus our attention on the external world, including our own external identity, and the endless drama of life. By turning inward, we find the real richness of life. There's gold within ourselves. It's like going gold digging within. To do this requires de-stimulation from the world of news, social media, and words. It requires us to turn down the volume of stimulation of the world around us to enter into that state.

When we lower the volume on all the stimulation in the world, then it is easy to be introspective. It's almost impossible to be introspective if you are watching three hours of TV every night or hours of mindless YouTube videos. You have to lower the volume on stimulation so you can hear what's spiritual. It is raising the volume of the spiritual. It's a quiet state in which you are raising the volume of what's real, what's beautiful, and what's eternal within you.

Introspection requires faith that what is inside is beautiful. There's a treasure inside, and it's worth digging for that treasure. People are afraid to go within because they are attached to what is outside and therefore cling to it. Also, most people are afraid to go within because they think they'll find their dark side and that it might overpower their beauty. What I've realized is that the darkness and the shadow are just superficial. Beyond that, there is a huge treasure so enjoyable and beautiful to behold. All it requires is for us to have faith that we souls are innately beautiful creatures. This faith in our inner beauty helps begin the process of introspection.

Sometimes, one virtue can be used to strengthen another virtue. For example, to achieve introspection, we must be determined to create an inner sanctuary for introspection so we can discover what's inside. Have faith in your inner beauty.

MEDITATION ON
INTROSPECTION

True introspection happens when you access what's real and what's beautiful inside you. It comes when you live in the spirit. When you have deep conviction that your spirit is filled with peace and love, then you will go within and discover and experience it. So, have faith in your inner beauty, have faith that at your core you are eternal light.

To be introspective all we have to do is move away from the external world of activities and social media for a few moments. Let's practice by visualizing a glorious meadow of grass and flowers. Breathe in the gentle breeze and slowly release it and relax into yourself. For the next few moments, think of peace -- a peace where you are free from any kind of internal conflict. Allow this peace to permeate your being completely while still imagining yourself in this meadow. Feel yourself far, far away from your world, going deeper into peace.

Take this moment and empty your mind of any worries. Take another deep breath and release it while taking in the lovely fragrance of the flowers around you. You are beginning to feel the eternal you. You are a lovely, luminous light energy.

Take another deep breath and slowly release it, while feeling the cool grass with your fingers. You are totally one with nature and attuned to yourself and you are completely relaxed. You have come home to who you are, an innately beautiful being. You experience a pure vibration of sacred stillness within you. You are peace. You are joy.

In this introverted state, you understand that the more you come to this place of stillness within, the more gifts you discover within yourself.

Om Shanti – I am Peace.

KINDNESS

Receiving an act of kindness at the right time can make or break a person. Kindness is such an important virtue, yet it is very often overlooked. It's an easy virtue to practice because all it requires on our part is some good wishes and pure feelings for the other person. When you have pure feelings, an act of kindness becomes easy, and it can make a huge difference in someone's life. For you, it might be a small gesture, but for the other person, it might really create something that helps them progress in life.

Just think about how many times you were going through something, and someone did something kind or supportive, and how uplifting it was for you. Kindness nourishes people—both the giver and the recipient—especially when that kindness comes from a genuine place. Kindness means tuning into people's feelings to see how they are doing and to wish them well. This happens when we find love inside ourselves and extend that love to the other.

Kindness is an under-valued virtue, especially in this day and age where everyone seems to be rushing about and looking out for themselves. Kindness is the opposite. We look and see what the other person needs in this moment.

MEDITATION ON
KINDNESS

by Bebe Butler (1974 – 2016)

There is a story about a mythical swan, and this swan's magic power is that it is able to select the pearls on the shore instead of stones. In the same way, the practice of kindness requires that I select and only pick up in my mind, the pure positive qualities of the people around me. Just like that mythical swan, I may see the defects their negative qualities sitting along the shore of their life, but I can choose not to focus on those.

There is a wisdom to kindness that knows, if I see negative qualities in others, two things will happen, my heart will harden, but I also run the risk of catching that quality ~ that defect. So the practice of kindness means that I focus on other people's pure qualities knowing that keeps the heart soft and the soul safe.

In my mind right now, I emerge one person who I may have conflict with, who I may have trouble seeing the goodness in, and I bring them in front of me in my mind. And, like that swan that picks up the pearls, I choose to focus right now on one beautiful quality in that person. Let me see that quality emanating from them in my mind. And, let me have appreciation for that quality. And as I look at them I see them as more than just a body, more than a role they play, but I see them as a soul, emanating that pure quality, that pearl of virtue that they have within them. And, I notice how my heart softens, how it expands, how I return to a deeper sense of peace and ease in my own being.

I notice how kindness brings more light into my own mind. And, I decide that the next time I see this person, the next time I have a conversation with this person, I will be like that mythical swan.

I will keep my focus on their good qualities, on their light, on that pure quality within their soul. The practice of kindness softens the heart, brings ease to the mind. There is also the other magical effect of kindness, and just like if I focus on a defect I will catch it, in the same way, when I focus on people's pure qualities, and pick up the pearls instead of the stones within them, I too will begin to radiate those pure qualities. I will begin to feel a sense of belonging, connectedness, and love for the world around me.

So, today, I will let go of being so harsh with the people around me. I will be like that mythical swan and see the stones along the shore but choose instead to focus and hold in my mind, the vision of the pure qualities of each person I come in contact with. This vision is a huge act of kindness towards others. It meets their deepest need to be seen for who they truly are.

Om Shanti – I am Peace.

RESILIENCE

Resilience is our ability to return to our original state of joy no matter what life throws at us. With resilience, we enjoy the present moment and pour love into every task no matter what transpired in the past.

When you stretch a strong rubber band, it returns to its original shape. If it's weak, overexposed to heat, or too old, then when you stretch it, it breaks. It doesn't go back to its original shape. In the same way, a healthy, strong soul is resilient. Innately we are all like strong rubber bands. Research in positive psychology has shown that resilience is intrinsic to everyone.

Research has shown that we each have a psychological immune system that helps us correct an emotional imbalance that robs us of happiness. Just as the body's immune system helps us fight disease, similarly each one of us has a psychological immune system that enables us to synthesize happiness from whatever is happening to us. In essence, we all have the capacity to find meaning and synthesize happiness even out of seemingly horrible events. By regularly unplugging from the world and going into our soul space, we can boost our psychological immune system.

Just as we prepare for a major physical storm, so, we must plan for inner storms. Challenges in life, like physical calamities, will come `but if we have a plan, if we have a daily spiritual practice, then very quickly, we can change the skies of our inner world to clear, calm, and beautiful. Resilience is also the capacity to see the rainbow at the end of the storm. It is facing challenges with strength and courage and being transformed through them.

MEDITATION ON
RESILIENCE

by Bebe Butler (1974 - 2016)

I take a few slow deep breaths inhaling and exhaling, and I prepare to experience my real being. I travel in my mind to a beautiful mountain at sunset. And I sit in the soft feathery grass and as I sit here it's as if the mountain holds my weight and absorbs any stress I have in my body. As I sit here, I enjoy the stillness of the sky: the quietude and the solitude. I enjoy being far away from the world and yet very close to home, very close to my real personality of peace. I can feel this right now, the serenity and the strength and I know that this solitude gives me the power to be resilient in the face of challenges. True resilience means that I face challenges without being jaded by them. It means I face challenges and I am reborn through those challenges.

When I give myself the experience of solitude then I become refreshed, and I am able to face challenges with wisdom, with power, with silence. But I also need the power to go within and ask myself, "What is one thing that I could do daily, spiritually to grow and face the challenges with more power, with more peace, with more stamina?" And, I sit and listen for that answer. And, just as I need to prepare for any major storm that I would experience in the physical world, in the same way when inner storms of life come, if I have a plan, if I have a daily spiritual effort or practice, then very quickly I'm able to change the skies of my inner world back to the ways they once were—clear, beautiful and peaceful.

With solitude and with the clear plan I am able to develop resilience, I am able to become as strong as the mountain that I am sitting on right now. And, like the blossom that remains trapped beneath the snow for nine to ten months, I also have an urge to grow. I also will find my way up into the air; I will find my way to blossom despite any challenge I may face. I too have the same urge to grow, to be the beautiful person, that I am destined to become. And, when these challenges come, I do not fear them or think of them as burdens, but I think of them as the chance to be reborn, to become wiser, to become more spiritually beautiful.

I take a deep breath, and I leave this beautiful place of solitude with an intention of creating a plan for my life spiritually so that I can be reborn through any challenge I may face and so that I may develop true spiritual resilience.

Om Shanti – I am Peace.

SERENITY

When I think of serenity, I envision a calm, still mountain lake. A serene person lives peacefully in the world but has few commentaries and opinions about what's going on. There's a refreshing stillness about their presence. They don't worry too much. They are not caught up in the future or the past. They have a natural trust that all will be well and that the soul is always safe.

Serenity requires us not to worry about the future. A serene being understands that the more one lives in the soul, the more one will be taken care of and supported. Such a person trusts that everything they need will come to them. A serene mind is a simple, clean mind that refreshes other people.

It's an easy virtue to practice in little moments. It doesn't have to be for long stretches at a time. One can effectively practice serenity even for five minutes. The key is to keep the mind easy and simple. Serenity is easy to lose and easy to get it back. It is one of the more accessible virtues and a gateway virtue. By practicing this virtue, we will acquire many other virtues.

MEDITATION ON
SERENITY

Serenity means not overthinking. Our mind is at rest because we are not worrying about the future or feeling guilty about the past. We are not grappling with any issues; our mind is easy, simple and in the now. You attain serenity by trusting—trusting all will be well and that you are safe.

Imagine a still mountain lake at dusk. There is a full moon out. Rays of the moonlight are dancing delicately across the lake. You are enchanted by the expanse of shimmering dark blue that lays before you.

Breathe in the fresh mountain air and become as still as the waters before you. Let yourself soak in the stillness and slowly and gently connect with your spiritual center.

You are safe; you are protected; you are light. Your spiritual core has infinite wisdom, and this wisdom is telling you all will be well.

You are as calm as this mountain lake. You are as fresh as this air. You are as luminous as this moonlight. You are perfect the way you are. Say to yourself gently but firmly, "I completely accept everything around me the way it is."

Your mind is as simple and easy as the atmosphere around this mountain lake. Keep repeating to yourself, "I am as serene as these waters. I trust whatever I need, will come to me. I am serene. I am serene."

This awareness of being in the moment and trusting that whatever you need, will come to you nourishes the soul to its core. It relaxes your nerves, and you feel serene.

Om Shanti – I am Peace.

SPONTANEITY

Once a motivational speaker was giving tips on how to come out of our comfort zones. She was saying how we get stuck in "ought to" and "supposed to," or on how we are supposed to behave, and how we are supposed to talk, and on how we fear going beyond our comfort zone. She was saying there's a five-second rule to breaking our comfort zones. Let's say you are at a gathering of people and you are drawn to talk to someone, then you have five seconds to act on that inspiration. In five seconds, if we are not spontaneous and push our comfort zone, then we are unlikely to free ourselves from our comfort zone.

Spontaneity is being able to act on intuitive feelings. Acting on our inspirations leads us out of the box into a more creative, zesty way of living. If you don't act on them, you stay in your old, dry comfort zone, doing the same thing again and again, and life becomes very blah. You never know what might happen by following an inspiration and just letting yourself be spontaneous. Spontaneity opens the door to a little bit more joy in life.

Spontaneity requires that we observe our thoughts. We also must be honest with ourselves. If we have a vague or explicit feeling something is not right with our lives, then seizing that thought and trying something different—that is spontaneity. To sustain spontaneity, we not only have to watch carefully to see when the impulses appear, but we also have to approach them with wisdom. Sometimes you can even ask yourself, "What can I do today to get out of my comfort zone?" "What piece of wisdom can I reflect on?" I could do something different in meditation. The change could be something simple such as stretching while we meditate. Spontaneity leads us into a space of variety, freshness, and freedom.

A word of caution here about spontaneity: Some people enjoy the thrill of roller coaster rides. They are free to enjoy these adventures because they feel safe and protected by the various security measures built into the amusement. Similarly, we are free to enjoy life's adventures and thrills when we take proper security measures that guarantee we will not hurt ourselves, or even self-destruct as we pursue life's thrills and adventures. Spontaneity is a virtue that needs to be cultivated with a lot of safety measures. There are basic principles we must follow, but within those principles we can be spontaneous.

MEDITATION ON
SPONTANEITY

To experience spontaneity in our lives, all we have to do is observe our thoughts, and in as many moments as possible, reflect on wisdom. So, let's begin by releasing from our minds the world of phones and social media and responsibilities and enter into that peace that is our true nature. Take a nice slow breath and slowly release it.

Let go of the world of struggle. Allow yourself to relax and release any subtle forms of "trying to make things happen." For the next few minutes, simply breathe in and out at your own natural pace. Notice the breath as it passes in and out... in and out... in and out... no need to visualize or make anything happen. Simply notice the breath and sense it moving through you as you relax into the moment.

Now shift your focus to observing what you are thinking. Continue to observe your thoughts; don't judge them, don't analyze them – just continue to observe them. Now accept and love each thought that comes. Love the random thoughts, the conflicting thoughts, the perverse ones, and the peaceful ones. Observing and loving your thoughts is a form of deep listening. The ability to be spontaneous is within all of us, we just have to deeply listen to what's going on inside us.

Now, ask yourself, "Who am I without these thoughts? Who am I without my history, without my story?" You sense that this story of your life is temporary there is an eternal part of you. In this state of true listening, you feel connected to the essence of who you really are. You sense the eternal soul that exists beyond the history. You think, "I am peace. I am conscient. I am light and free." Reflecting on such wisdom quenches your mind and stills it.

Ideas begin to come to you from the quietude of your mind. Your mind is dancing like the wind and you feel the freedom within. It has gone into full spontaneous mode. From this place of serenity, you understand that any spontaneous step is the right step. Every random thought is sweet joy, it blossoms into a spontaneous action. You deeply know every thought from this soul space will take you out of your comfort zone it will help you grow and mature.

Om Shanti – I am Peace.

WITNESS

According to quantum mechanics, particles do not take on formal properties until we observe or measure them. Until then, they can exist simultaneously in two or more places. Once measured, however, they snap into a more classical reality, existing in only one place. This shows us that in some important ways, the physical world is a joint product of the observer and the observed.

Being a witness means that we silently watch life from the vantage point of an observer. We remain uninfluenced, true to our higher self, and aligned with qualities like serenity, love, and joy.

Being a witness grounds us and connects us to that which is true and eternal. It frees us from the shackles of limiting beliefs and from the pulling of our own or another's false ego. When we act as a witness, our universe subtly shifts and we become co-creators of reality. This special power of acting as a detached observer allows us to dive into our innermost being and emerge with profound existential insights.

Then we begin to observe ourselves. This means we don't create stories or make up ideas about what we are doing or who we are. We don't worry about what a particular situation means about us. Just watch yourself like you would watch a train or car pass, almost the way a little child watches the clouds and birds move through the sky. Just as a child doesn't worry about the birds or clouds, so we should turn off our constantly rumbling, analyzing mind and just witness everything. By listening in silence, we allow a different type of learning to take place. This learning is not based on actively creating ideas but rather on receiving understanding through observation and silence. Being a witness is a way to tune in, observe, and listen to the world.

Witness is an easy virtue to practice. It is a gateway virtue. It's a foundational virtue. The foundational ones like silence and witness give rise to the complex virtues. They give power to the more advanced virtues.

MEDITATION ON
WITNESS

To truly experience freedom from limiting beliefs, to remain uninfluenced and access inner power, we must act as observers. To observe clearly, we need to first detach ourselves and then create a still space in our mind. For this, we have to let go of our inner and outer chatter.

We will first become a witness to our thoughts, then of ourselves, and then of the dramas around us. So, take a moment now and become an observer of where you are sitting, the city, the room, your immediate surroundings. Observe yourself sitting there for a few moments. Now gently but firmly, let go of any stresses you have, let go of your roles. Turn your attention to your breath. Simply observe your breath going in and out—in and out—in and out.

Imagine you are riding a glass elevator up, up and away, away from the world, way up into the sky. Beyond the physical universe, beyond the Milky Way, beyond the galaxies, as you go up, you are beginning to feel lighter.

You have arrived in a beautiful misty region of white light. You feel totally light here. Now, ask yourself the question, "What am I thinking?" Just be a witness to what comes to your mind. Don't judge, just keep observing your thoughts. Now, ask yourself the question, "If I had a choice, what would I be thinking instead of what I am thinking now?" Keep observing your thoughts, your feelings in response to this question. Witness any visuals that come to your mind. Just keep watching your mind as you would watch cars go by. Keep watching the traffic in your mind without judgment.

Now, again get in the elevator of consciousness and go even higher. Go beyond any reach of the physical universe. Allow your soul to become light as a feather and even more silent. You are now in an ocean of golden orange light that feels cool and welcoming. You feel at home here. It is feels like your personal haven. You are in a sanctuary of silence.

Now, ask yourself this question, "Who am I?" 'Who am I?" and again observe. Observation is like deep listening. Observe your thoughts, observe your feelings. Are any visuals coming up? And, again go back to the question, "Who am I really?" Notice your response to that.

Now, look down on your life below on earth and observe your life. Observe the people in your life, your work, your relationships. Just watch like you are watching a movie. Ask yourself this question, "What is meaningful in my life?" Witness the thoughts and feelings that are coming up in response to that question. "What are the visuals? What is meaningful in my life?"

When we detach and become a witness from a place of peace, we gain invaluable insights. Gently take the elevator back toward the room you are sitting in. Coming back into the world of sights and sounds you really understand the quote: You are not a human being in search of a spiritual experience. You are a spiritual being immersed in a human experience.

Sense yourself as a soul in that physical body, playing a part on the world stage.

Om Shanti – I am Peace.

INTERMEDIATE VIRTUES

AUTHENTICITY

Authenticity happens when you are willing to be your real self wherever you are at any given moment. It is authentic to allow people to see who you really are—warts and all. It can only happen if you let go of your attachment to your image.

As this implies, we all have an authentic, true spiritual self. In our daily life, sometimes we are in a high consciousness, we are connected, and sometimes we just have a lot of gunk coming up in our mind. All of us without exception go through these variations. So why are we anxious to hide it? It is because we get programmed into thinking, "Be strong, be impressive, be in control." We feel that other people must think that we are doing well, that we have it all figured out. We try to hide our vulnerabilities and weaknesses, lest others take advantage or have bad opinions of us. We create a lot of stress for ourselves when we try to project an image or hide something.

Life gets trickier when you are playing a role. The question arises, when is the right moment to be vulnerable? When should we share intimate things? It is not that we should pour our heart out to everyone. But, we don't have to hide everything either. This is about taking off the armor and having the courage to be whoever you really are and allowing your true self to be seen. If you allow yourself to be seen wherever you are then, your true authentic self will emerge. What blocks our true authentic self from emerging is our unwillingness to be vulnerable. Once you are willing to be seen as imperfect and you let go of your ego image that wants people to see you a certain way, only then can you see your inner light. You reach your light through your vulnerability and by consciously doing the exercises in this book.

The practice of letting yourself be seen in your weakness and lower moments, combined with a meditative practice of holding your highest vision of yourself—these two together are essential to nurture your authenticity. You can't just know your light; you have to know your darkness. You can't just feel and see your light; you have to be comfortable when you are seen in your weakness, too. This is what makes us feel connected to each other, because we are not merely pretending to be authentic.

MEDITATION ON
AUTHENTICITY

Finding our authenticity means discovering our whole self, both the divine part of us and the vulnerable part of us. It is not only about learning who we truly are, but also learning who we are meant to be. For this, we have to be willing to be seen as imperfect and let go of our ego image that wants to be seen a certain way. Authenticity involves seeing your light and your darkness. It is about not pretending we are anything other than our true, real self.

Take a few moments now and unplug from the world around you. Imagine that you are sitting overlooking a peaceful, calm lake at the break of dawn. The water is so still that the surface of the lake looks like perfect glass with hues of blue and grey. Slowly, as the sun rises over the lake, you notice a beautiful tableau of pink and copper. As you watch the world awaken, you are inspired to seek your authenticity.

Take a nice slow breath and while looking out at the grand vision in front of you; ask yourself the questions, "What is most meaningful to me in my life? What brings joy to my life?" Take another deep breath and breathe in the tranquility of the lake and the ambiance.

Keep reflecting on the questions, "What brings meaning to my life? What makes me truly happy?" Your authentic self can only express itself when you spend time in silent contemplation like this. The magnificence around you is a reflection of the beauty that lives inside of you. Just as the sun is shining on the lake bold and free, your light, your authentic self is brilliant. This is the real you.

In this silent space, be kind and gentle but firm with yourself and strip away your self-doubt. Strip away your insecurities. Ask yourself the question, "Who would I be without my resentments, without my baggage?" "Who would I be when all these things about me fade away?" See yourself in your vulnerable state. Give yourself permission to see your light and your darkness. Be present in this vulnerable state for a few moments.

Now imagine yourself, standing in front of this shimmering expanse of water and ask yourself the question, "When I strip away all my insecurities, what is left? Who am I without my limiting beliefs?"

This is the authentic you. Now, allow yourself to see yourself as more than just your physical form. Envision yourself as light, as spiritual energy. Just as the sun is shining a light on the world, shine a light on your real self—a spiritual being of light and love. This is your authentic self. Remember, authenticity means not to be afraid of our blemishes while radiating our beauty.

Om Shanti – I am Peace.

CLEANLINESS

Cleanliness requires daily maintenance. The perfect analogy here is housecleaning. If you think about it, you always have something to clean in your home. If you don't regularly tidy your house, it gets scary. Things pile up in corners for weeks, months, or even years. It becomes a disaster. In our context here, regular cleaning is your daily spiritual practice—observing where the mental clutter is and whisking it away. Just as you scan your house and put things in their place, so, you must be very vigilant to keep your mind and heart clean.

Both your mind and your heart have to be clean. The heart is most important. You can't hold negative things about people in your heart. Even if the other has done awful things to you, you must let it go for your own sake. If we hold a few grudges here and there, it oppresses our heart. It all begins when we notice a few micro-aggressions done against us. Soon after, our spirit begins to feel heavy.

A clean mind and heart treasure innocence and simplicity. There is a simplicity about clean people. For example, if you keep your house clean, you won't have tons of furniture and knick-knacks because you know that means more surfaces to dust. Similarly, simple, innocent minds do not keep unnecessary stuff in their thoughts. Once the mind gets too complicated and thinks of too many unpleasant interactions, it's hard to keep it clean.

We must work to overcome the force of laziness, in order to keep a daily maintenance routine of cleanliness going. It's something you have to keep doing again and again and again with attention. Keep watching your mind and drop the waste as soon as you notice it. Observe your mind and drop negative thoughts and opinions about something or someone that just bothered you.

Sometimes people tire of this daily maintenance because it feels like a lot of work. Remember, it's easier to do a little bit of cleaning each day than neglect it and end up with a very dirty soul that you have to struggle with down the road. Cleanliness requires regular baby steps.

MEDITATION ON
CLEANLINESS

Cleanliness is being a witness to your mind, observing where the junk is and letting it go. Think of it as a spiritual house cleaning service that you have to engage in yourself. To employ this service, we have to overcome complacency because to keep our hearts and minds clean requires daily maintenance. We have to keep doing it regularly with a lot of attention.

Imagine you are watching a powerful yet tranquil waterfall. There is a stillness around it as it roars down the rocks. Keep watching this streaming water as it tumbles down. This scene before you is compelling you to be a witness to your thoughts. Keep watching your mind, make a mental note of the thoughts you are having. Ask yourself the question; this thought I just had, is it necessary? Do I really need to think this thought right now? If you think it is a useless thought, then let it go. Visualize yourself standing under the waterfall. As the water is pouring over you, you feel it washing away your waste thoughts.

Again, become an observer of your mind. Ask yourself the question, "Am I holding any negative opinions of situations or people?" Now, envision yourself under the tranquil but cleansing waterfall. The force of the water as it cascades over you is powerfully scrubbing your mind of negative opinions and emotions.

Be still for a few moments and keep watching your mind. Now ask yourself the questions, "Am I holding any grudges against anyone? Am I playing the blame game?" Again, step under the waterfall and let the water descend over you, washing away any vestiges of negativity from your mind. The cascades of water are cleansing your heart of all negativity.

To keep the heart and mind clean, we shouldn't even have opinions of something we just saw. To cultivate cleanliness, we have to do this exercise daily. The daily self-cleaning service might seem like a lot of work. But, remember, it's easier to do a little bit of cleaning each day than neglecting it and having a huge dirty soul that you have to address down the road.

Om Shanti – I am Peace.

Refer to page 70 for the link to free audios of all the meditations featured in this book.

CONCENTRATION

Concentration happens when we are focused and unavailable for distractions, when we are single-minded and clear, and especially when we allow ourselves to be totally alone with our inner work. It's creating a workshop for ourselves, like an artist's studio or a chemist's lab. Similarly, to concentrate, we must create an inner space for ourselves where we enter and are undistracted, and where we can just focus solely on our spiritual work. It could be a thought or an exercise; it's taking that time for solitude and silence and just being and doing that one thing instead of a million other things.

Developing concentration is pretty simple; all we have to do is hold one thought and stay on it with inner solitude. By taking short periods during the day and focusing on spiritual work, we develop concentration. Be totally unavailable for distractions during those few moments because it is so easy to want to answer the phone or check Instagram or... It is not just external distractions but also internal distractions. For example thinking, this person said this or I have to do this. "What should I have for dinner? Why didn't this happen? Why did this person do this."

To develop concentration, you have to be very firm with yourself and not entertain any distractions. There should just be this one thought, right now this is my focus. There should be focus, but without stress.

This kind of peaceful attention will help you focus your concentration on truths that will take you to a high spiritual place.

MEDITATION ON
CONCENTRATION

Concentration happens when I create a spiritual workshop for myself. Let's create an inner space for ourselves. We have to be firm with ourselves in this space. Don't allow any distractions. Think of it as your personal lab in which you will be single-minded and clear, just as a scientist would. This inner space is where you can focus solely on your spiritual work. Now, let's take a set of four pure thoughts as our spiritual exercise. When I make time for solitude and focus on a collection of pure thoughts and keep looping these thoughts in my mind instead of a million other things, then I develop concentration.

To help us concentrate we need a set of what I call "go-to pure thoughts." These thoughts will help you focus. My go-to pure thoughts are:

- *I am spirit. I am an eternal being of light.*

- *I am pure and innocent. This is my original nature.*

- *I, the soul, come to this world to experience the adventure of the physical dimension.*

- *I am spiritual energy. My time in this material world is coming to an end. It is time for me, the soul, to go back to my spiritual home.*

You can make this meditation personal by picking 3 or 4 pure thoughts that speak to you. Take a moment to establish yourself in your sequence of pure thoughts. Remember they have to be pure, eternal thoughts. Then keep looping them in your mind without giving in to any external thoughts through the whole of the sequence. For example, if you have an outside thought ("What am I eating for dinner?"), then make a mental note of it and next time be firm with yourself and go through the sequence without any external thoughts. Use visualization and understanding to build your experience.

So, let's concentrate:

- *I take a moment and remember that I am spirit. I am an eternal being of light.*

- *My intrinsic nature is innocence.*

- *I, the soul, come to this world to experience the adventure of the physical dimension.*

- *I am spiritual energy. This body is my costume. It is time for me to shed my costume and return to my spiritual home.*

Keep going through the sequence four or five times. Affirm to yourself that you will keep looping this sequence of thoughts again and again in your mind. This kind of focused exercise helps you still your mind and concentrate.

Om Shanti – I am Peace.

FLEXIBILITY

Flexibility is the ability to adjust - our plans, our ideas, and even our attitude and vision. To develop this virtue, one needs to be able to let go of desires and preferences, be pretty content and happy with oneself.

Let's say, you had plans to go somewhere, and last minute there were changes, then you are okay. Or, you wanted a particular outcome in a situation, you would have liked it to go this way, but something else happened; you are okay. You accept that there is benefit and keep moving—you don't get stuck anywhere. This kind of flexibility comes from contentment, easiness, and lightness in the soul. Flexible people don't take their support from things going their way; they deeply understand that change is inevitable.

After making your best efforts, flexibility is the willingness to accept and flow with the outcome. It is realizing that what is, is the way to your spiritual destination. You adjust your expectations easily knowing that through your positive outlook your life begins to flow in the direction of your maximum growth.

Flexibility requires mental agility where you are not fixed in your own set pattern of thinking and doing. There is an openness to new ways of doing things and thinking about things. Actually, there is not just openness, but there is a sense of adventure.

One of the ways in which we can look at life is that it is a game. When you see some aspects of your life as a game, then you stay calm and unflustered through the many dramas of life. You see each situation as an opportunity to stay in your soul or to practice a power. You acknowledge there's wisdom to things not going your way. You see wisdom in surprises. Remember life is a gift and an amazingly enjoyable adventure if you are willing to flex. This is an intermediate virtue, which is not too difficult.

MEDITATION ON
FLEXIBILITY

Flexibility is suppleness of mind. It is about not being stuck but to look at life with fresh eyes, unconditioned, and willing to learn. For this, we need to remember two secrets: One is to trust in the intelligence of the universe, and the other is to keep renewing ourselves.

To recharge yourself, you don't have to go anywhere except inside yourself, away from the physical world of form and sound. Taking a vacation from the physical world helps us to become fluid.

Now take a moment and visualize a beautiful still starlit night. This night sky is like a piece of art. It is whispering to your spirit to become very still. Take a deep breath and become as peaceful as this evening sky. Allow it to permeate your being as you breathe in and become as still as the vastness of the sky before you. Soak in this stillness and slowly and gently connect with your spiritual energy within.

You are spirit. You are light. In your center, you are flexible and easy going. Detach from the world of form and keep in your awareness, "I am. I am spirit. I just am. I am as still as this night sky." This awareness that you are a soul and you are sacred renews the soul to its core. It relaxes you, and you feel supple.

Now, take a moment and look at the vastness of the night sky. With your mind's eye gently pull a curtain back to reveal a mysterious and magical universe. To be flexible in addition to renewing ourselves, we need to trust in the wisdom of the universe before us. Talk to yourself, "I may not agree with some aspects of what is going on right now but let me accept. I accept because I understand that the outcome can be benevolent." Remember the times in your life, when your greatest pains turned to your greatest gifts. So instead of labeling things as good or bad, instead of resisting the change around you, trust in its destination. Take a deep breath now and accept everything and everyone around you as it is and as they are.

Change is an inevitable part of life. There has never been a night that hasn't given way to a beautiful dawn. Easiness comes when you go into silence and become aware of the wisdom of this wonderful universe. Flexibility is making all storms into gifts because each storm brings strength and illumination.

Om Shanti – I am Peace.

INTEGRITY

Integrity is to be true to oneself while honoring one's commitments to others. We have integrity when our speaking and doing match, when we live by our conscience and do the right thing however long it takes. People trust a person with integrity. If you live with integrity, people know that your word is your bond.

Integrity also has authenticity. It means we speak our mind. We don't just speak whatever enters our mind. Rather, we are honest, we are open, and we clearly express ourselves without fear of other people's judgments.

Integrity also entails honesty. Those with integrity are upright and free from deceit. The best adage that exemplifies this is: An honest day's work. You keep the integrity of your word and the integrity of your actions intact.

There are two types of integrity. There is integrity based on following a moral code set by culture and community. And, there is the integrity of following our conscience. The second comes from a pure space of commitment to do what's right in our life. To achieve this state, we must continually show up, choosing what's right even when it's difficult. Also, the second aspect of integrity pushes you out of your comfort zone and challenges you.

There aren't any hidden agendas with integrity. There's no hidden manipulation, our motives are pure, and our decisions come from our conscience. Our words are sincere without being harsh or harmful. We are responsibly and helpfully honest, not brutally honest.

MEDITATION ON
INTEGRITY

Integrity is a way of being in which our words and actions match a high code of conduct. Their word is their bond for people who are in integrity. Integrity is not doing anything against our conscience; however much we feel pressured. More than anything else, a person in integrity will always perform actions from an undiluted space of sincerity, honor, and fairness.

Take a few moments now and unplug from the world around you. Imagine that you are sitting overlooking a peaceful, calm lagoon at dawn. The water is so still that the surface of the lagoon looks like a mirror, reflecting the color of the blue grey sky above. Slowly, as the sun rises over the lagoon, you notice a beautiful tapestry of copper hues. As you watch the world awaken you are inspired to seek integrity.

Take a nice slow breath and look out at the grand vision in front of you. Take another deep breath and breathe in the tranquility of the lagoon and the ambiance. The magnificence around you is a reflection of the conscience that lives inside of you. Your inner voice can only be accessed in moments of contemplation and solitude like this. Just as the sun is shining on the water bold and free, your conscience is brave and waiting to see the light of day.

In this silent space, give yourself permission to see your conscience and live in your conscience. Tell yourself, no matter what, I will follow what I feel is right and true. Even though some actions may seem expedient, you understand that in the long run, they will cost your soul. They will slowly but surely erode your self-trust.

Just as the sun is shining a light on the world, shine a light on your inner code of conduct. You understand that to bring health to your heart, your code of conduct has to be based on honor. You accept that your words have to match your actions. More than anything else, the things that have enduring value are our actions done in integrity. Just like the brilliant sun shining on the lagoon in front of you, actions done with a pure motive, with honesty, and with trustworthiness are the ones that shine bright.

Take a deep breath and slowly release this breath and promise yourself, that you will live by honor and integrity. No matter what the cost, you will live by your conscience with honesty.

Om Shanti – I am Peace.

PATIENCE

When people say patience is a virtue, they speak the truth! Patience is a combination of power and peace. Patience allows everything to come in its own time. It is the power not to rush, push, or to slow down. Patience is waiting for us when we go deeper and trust more deeply.

Some virtues help other virtues. Trust helps patience. We need trust that everything will come at its own time, trust that we can't always hasten something by rushing it or pushing it. Impatience comes from fear.

Consider a plant. You want it to grow quickly, but you can only give it so much water and fertilizer. You can't give more and expect it to grow any faster than its natural rhythm. In fact, you will harm the plant. You must let it grow at its own pace. To achieve patience, we need to understand the rhythm of things, of people, of actions, and interactions. There is a rhythm to life, and that rhythm will ultimately prevail. It will also end in everyone's benefit. To understand that rhythm and to flow with that rhythm is patience.

You need enough peace inside yourself to be willing to go slowly with things that you cannot accelerate. Just take a deep breath and slow down when things are not going at the pace you wanted. Learn to have that soft spot of stillness within and allow yourself to rest while things come in their own time.

MEDITATION ON
PATIENCE

More than just being a virtue, patience in today's fast-paced world is an essential skill. Patience involves a mixture of acceptance and understanding. There is a wisdom in knowing that all things have a rhythm and flowing with that rhythm. When we work from a place of peace and not ego, then we can cultivate patience. Patience brings a joyful purpose to our lives.

Let's first relax into our bodies. Take a deep breath and while releasing this breath relax your legs. You're relaxed. Take another deep breath and release this breath and relax your stomach area. You're even more relaxed. Take another deep breath and release this breath slowly and relax your shoulders and arms. You're feeling totally relaxed.

In this state of relaxation, you are connected to your core being, to the real you... You are an eternal peaceful soul... In this space, you are no longer impatient or annoyed, you are the peaceful true you. Now take a situation that usually makes you impatient. It could be traffic, or behavior of your co-worker, or something else on a national or international scale. Acknowledge your feelings. Gently but firmly, divert your attention to being a peaceful eternal soul. Keep seeing yourself as a serene spirit. Now, retake a look at the situation, it is starting to become easier to accept the situation or the person for what it is and who they are. Keep repeating to yourself, "I accept. I accept. I accept."

Take another deep breath. Continue to breathe deeply while observing your thoughts. Slowly align your thoughts to your breath. As you watch yourself breathe in and out, tell yourself, "There is a rhythm to everything in life. I can't control the rhythm, but I can allow myself to flow with it. I accept I can't make it go any faster than it already is. This is the way of life, and I accept it."

Keep breathing deeply in and out, in and out, in and out. You are beginning to feel calm and patient. This, in turn, is increasing your trust. You trust that all will be well. You understand that gradually things will turn out for everyone's benefit.

Keep breathing in and out and keep watching your breath. You feel so serene. In this state, you understand that everything changes and with humility you embrace change. By allowing your thoughts and breath to come into harmony, you have learned the crucial skill of patience.

Om Shanti – I am Peace.

SILENCE

Spiritual silence is a harmony of the mind, intellect, and body. There is harmony in your inner being, and that harmony creates silence in the soul. Silence means to be free of useless thoughts and desires. There is no conflict, and no cacophony in the mind. The soul can't be in deep silence for too long, but we can experience moments of it. Serenity leads to silence.

Serenity is stillness while moving within the world, whereas silence is the ability to completely go beyond it and just experience the soul space in a very simple form — existing as light in connection with the Source. In silence, there is nothing of this world, no sound, no visual images, just pure existence, completely beyond sound. It is the experience of complete nirvana. Again, serenity is moving in the world with tranquility, acting in the world yet free of chatter and commentary. Silence is a little more profound and beyond.

To enter silence, you need to be very pure. The soul has to be very pure, and our consciousness has to be very clean in order to experience silence. We must be transparent, and then the soul will become silent. Silence requires a lot of discipline. It takes determination to break the habit of getting caught up in the world of sound and form.

We can all take baby steps toward silence. I once saw an Oprah show where some people became millionaires by just saving all their change over many years. Whatever change they got back from a transaction they would collect, and it eventually built up into huge savings for them.

We can take baby steps of silence by practicing it in as many moments as possible. Silence does not require thinking, or sitting down for two hours of meditation, but rather, learning the art of increasing the minutes.

MEDITATION ON
SILENCE

Silence is so much more than just quietness; it is living in complete harmony with the soul. It is the experience of just being you, a peaceful soul. In silence you feel timeless, your presence feels absolute and only this moment is all there is. Silence nurtures the soul, brings joy, a timeless wisdom, and a sacred love. There is more synergy, more nourishment, and more prosperity in our lives.

So, let's prepare to go into silence by switching off our desires, our analytical mind. Shine a light on your worry, any confusions, your desires, over analyses and switch that light off. When you switch this light off, you banish them from your conscious mind.

Imagine a gorgeous sunset on the ocean. Steady your gaze on the horizon as you watch the sun, a luminous ball of golden orange, slowly dip below it. Now, breathe deeply in and out, in and out, in and out. Your breath is slowing, your thoughts are slowing, your body begins to feel relaxed, and you lose yourself in this moment and in this sunset.

The rays of the sun are washing over you. Breathe in and exhale, breathe in and exhale and as you do you feel yourself again relax twice as deeply. Your body is beginning to feel weightless. As the rays of the sun are cleansing you, you enter into the sacred place of the soul, into deep peace. This is your original nature.

You are light. You are peace. Again, take a deep breath, breathing in slowly and breathing out as you again double your stillness and go even deeper into sweet silence. You feel totally weightless; you are nothing but pure light. In this stillness, nothing changes and time has no power. Allow this silence to slip inside of you, allow the silence to fill inside of you and emanate from inside of you. Continue to absorb this energy of silence.

This silence is so much more than just quietness, you are in complete harmony with yourself and with the world around you. You feel open and free and resourceful. Now, take a few more moments to remember who you are, "I am light. I am peace. I am clear and pure."

In this silence, it is clear to you that you only have the present. You understand that you have to make this moment count by filling it with silence to make your future powerful, to make your external life harmonious. You affirm to yourself that daily as soon as you get up and before you go to bed you will do this exercise. Breathing in and breathing out slowly and deeply you come back feeling recharged and restored.

Om Shanti – I am Peace.

STABILITY

Stability is the ability to anchor yourself in the soul and take your power and peace from your true self. When you learn to ride a bike, or drive a car, you must carefully focus at first, and then it becomes natural. In the same way, the soul develops stability when it becomes natural to anchor oneself in soul space. When you've anchored yourself again and again, then no matter what goes on you know you can re-anchor to your center because you've done it so many times.

Stability develops within the soul by the practice of anchoring. It becomes so subconscious and natural that we cannot be hijacked out of our center. We will always know how to get back to our center.

For example, when you learn to ride a bike, you try to find your center of gravity so you can stay on the bike. It's the same with spiritual knowledge. You have to use spiritual knowledge to find your center in both meditation and action. You use your wisdom to keep steady and to stay on course. We are learning to ride the bike of life without getting distracted and derailed.

This requires serious focus. For example, even if you fall off a bike, you pick yourself up and keep going. Stability also helps to keep riding the bike of life. All of us are going to lose it sometimes, and stability helps us get back on and keep riding. Stability here means to keep at it and not give up on yourself. When you achieve stability, you do not give up on a task once undertaken. Nor do you give up on others. Stability requires us to be sensitive, and observant of when we go off track so that we can find a way to bring ourselves back on our path.

MEDITATION ON
STABILITY

Stability comes from anchoring in our wisdom. It is the art of being solid and constant while going through the ups and downs of life. Stability requires us to have equanimity while coming into relationships. It comes from understanding that we are all going to lose it now and then, but to be focused, so we don't get hijacked away from our center.

Sit up straight and take a few deep breaths and release them slowly. Mentally do a scan of your body. Notice if you are holding any tension in any part of your body. It could be your shoulders, your stomach area, or anywhere else. Now breathe in deeply, visualizing that breath going to that tense part of your body.

Hold the breath there for a few seconds and release the breath while relaxing that part of your body. Let's do it again. Take a deep breath, imagining you are sending oxygen going to another tense part of your body. Hold the breath there for a few seconds and release it while relaxing it. Take another deep breath, hold it for a few seconds and release it while decompressing and relaxing your whole body.

Now, imagine light energy traveling from your feet to your stomach area to your shoulders and then to the center of your forehead. While this light energy is progressing up your body, it is diffusing all your stresses, and you are becoming more and more calm. Now, focus your light energy in the center of your forehead. As you stay focused, there is a powerful feeling of centeredness. You understand that this is your spiritual center of gravity.

Now, become aware of any negative emotions you are holding inside of yourself. Slowly take a deep breath and while releasing that breath release those emotions. See yourself as light, a luminous star in the center of the forehead. This star is you. This is also your spiritual center. This visualization of being light is filling your center with power and equanimity.

Bring to mind a relationship or situation that makes you fall off the bike of life – a time when you don't feel steady. Now, replace that scene in your mind's eye and see yourself as light energy. This is your core, your spiritual center of gravity. Keep coming back to this spiritual axis point because it steadies you on the bike of life. Daily practice of coming home to your true self helps you gain stability.

Om Shanti – I am Peace.

SWEETNESS

Sweetness is having only good things in our hearts and only kind thoughts in our minds. It means to feel softness and freshness in our interaction with the world and other people; not to feel jaded or cynical. When our nature becomes sweet, we don't draw attention to other's weaknesses. People with sweetness carry a highlighter that highlights the beauty in other people, and naturally highlights their virtues, their gifts, their sacredness. That vision sweetens their interactions with other people and enables them to look closely, but with love.

I recently met a two-year-old girl. She was so sweet that just by her presence, I felt sweetness. Her presence was so gentle, so sweet, so pleasing. It was also her innocence, her lack of guile, and the fact that she wasn't looking at what's wrong with the world or people.

When you become an adult, you understand motives, you notice agendas, and you risk becoming jaded. The deepest spiritual sweetness is to be aware of all such things and still not see them. As adults, we cannot be naive or indifferent to real problems such as climate change or gender inequality, but to keep our hearts clean while caring for the world is sweetness. Sweet people possess an extraordinary spiritual fragrance because they are seeing and highlighting goodness.

Real sweetness is the result of a long journey inward to our core, to the fountain of virtue. It comes from continually sipping from and bathing in this fountain. It comes from developing a positive attitude under all circumstances over a long period of time. There is a timelessness to sweetness, and it is a virtue we acquire when we have experienced eternity.

MEDITATION ON
SWEETNESS

There is a profound wisdom to sweetness. The wisdom to take the road less traveled and not be cynical, the wisdom to hold a positive attitude no matter the circumstance, and, most importantly, the wisdom to love in a pure way. Sweetness empowers the self and others and gives birth to innocence.

Let's develop this quality of sweetness. Slowly breathe in and out. Again, breathe in and out as you move deeply into your center. With each breath, allow yourself to go deeper and deeper into that quiet center within. Imagine that deep inside you there is a switch that can turn off all the chatter and noise of the mind. Turn this switch off now and relax into deep stillness.

Now, imagine you are sitting by a fountain in a luscious park. There is fresh air all around you. Imagine taking a sip from this fountain. The water tastes like sweet spring rain.

Take a sip of water and continue to breathe in and out deeply. Talk to yourself, "My nature is as sweet as this water. I'm innately good and pure." Take a deep breath and breathe in the sweet fragrance of the flowers all around you. There is a very special spiritual fragrance to you, too.

Take another deep breath and as you exhale, let the world of sound vanish, and you enter into a sweet, silent communion with yourself. In this stillness, you understand that you have a purpose. Your purpose is to drink from the fountain of virtue within you and to share that with others, to touch the light and to radiate those qualities into the world. Your purpose is to illumine the darkness of your mind and to replenish the fountain of sweetness within, so others can drink from it.

Take a moment now and see yourself and feel yourself as light and as spiritual energy. You are a spiritual being, an eternal light. This awareness brings you in connection with the Source, the Supreme eternal light. The Source of sweetness and silence. You are pulled into a luminous world of light. Let this beautiful world of silence and sweetness wash over you like a soft breeze as you absorb the gentle, comforting energy of the Divine. Allow yourself to let go and simply receive sweetness that is flowing through the atmosphere. Take your time and absorb this sweet energy of the Source.

As you absorb this energy, you begin to smile. There is a sweetness to your smile. You begin to feel like a ray of sunshine, light and easy. You are aware of everything, but you choose only to focus on the best aspects of it all. Your heart is dancing, your mind is calm, and you feel like a new rose in bloom.

By breathing in and out gently, return to your surroundings but vow to practice sweetness today; to sip from the sweet fountain within and see the beauty in each moment and each being.

Om Shanti – I am Peace.

TRUST

There are two aspects to trust. One is others trusting us, that is knowing: I am trustworthy. The second is us trusting someone or something. When I work on the first aspect, then the second aspect follows, with a little bit of effort. Being trustworthy is very deep. The more transparent I am in my interactions with others, the more I am trusted. When I say one thing and mean something else, or when my actions are not consistent with my words, then it is hard for people to trust me. When my actions are integrated with my principles, then not only will others trust me, but this trust will also bring their blessings to me.

In the second aspect of trust, we need to trust that situations will work out for our benefit; we have to trust our deep intuition, and we have to trust that God will take care of us, if we allow God to do this. A dedicated spiritual leader, Sister Mohini, once said, "Faith is of the intellect and trust is of the heart." When there is trust in the heart, then intuitively we know things will work out. Trust has enough power to make things work out. All these virtues have a specific power associated with them. They are not just intellectual exercises; they have an energy that moves things.

You may be thinking this all sounds too pat. What if you've had bad experiences with trust? The effort we have to make here is to again be like a child—a child of the Source. Just as when a child comes into the world, the child naturally trusts that the parent will take care of him/her. The child trusts that he/she will get food, love, and care. Trust happens when we go back to being a child of the Supreme Soul, understanding that God is trustworthy.

I love the motto of the United States of America, "In God we trust." This requires some intentionality and surrender. Let's begin our surrender to the benevolent Source, by saying aloud, "I trust. I trust. I trust You, Oh Divine One." Eventually, our heart will follow our words. This act of surrendering is reciprocated and gives us trust. A trusting soul draws, attracts things towards himself/herself; things start to work out.

Even though it's not always simple to become a child again, if you have the sincere intention to learn to trust, and you sincerely work toward it in relationship with the Source, then you will experience trust. Just the intention to understand and experience trust begins the process of achieving trust. This trust, in turn, helps me anchor my life in the eternal and unchanging truths of spirituality. I'm able to dance with all the external changes that are bound to happen in life. Trust gives strength and strength brings connection.

MEDITATION ON
TRUST

by Bebe Butler (1974 - 2016)

Because the heart has been hurt, I sometimes keep the doors of my heart locked. But right now, I allow those doors to open as I enter into the heart of my own, deeper, spiritual personality. Within me, there is a vast amount of love and a vast amount of peace. And when I spend time in this stillness, I can begin to plug into my own source of love and peace. I can begin to trust that there is an inner source of spiritual beauty.

I sense myself as just pure light. As the light that is loving, gentle, soft. And I allow the feeling of that gentleness to blossom in my being. When I connect with my own spiritual personality, it becomes easy to sense, to love the Supreme Being my spiritual Mother and to know that I am deeply loved and cared for by this Being. Though the world may come and go, and at times be inconsistent, the love of the Supreme is always constant. And the love within my being is always there. I only have to remember it, emerge it and experience it.

When I trust that the source of love can be found within me, I can release my feelings of distrust. And I can be more comfortable with the inconsistencies of those around me because I know that no one can actually take love away from me. Love is who I am. And love is what I find when I connect with my supreme Mother. This love makes me strong and fearless, and I can open the doors of my heart and allow others to experience the beautiful qualities of my inner being. I can trust that the love I need is within me and it will always be there.

Om Shanti – I am Peace.

# LINK TO FREE AUDIOS
for all the meditations featured in this book:

https://shireenchada.com/oh-my-goodness-audios/

ADVANCED VIRTUES

BALANCE

Spiritual balance is a perfect integration of two positives. For example, we learn to balance love and detachment, which are both positive. But if there isn't a perfect balance of loving someone and being detached, then, every time that person says something disagreeable, or has an off mood, I get upset. If there isn't healthy space between you and the other person, then true love is not possible. Hence, we have to be both loving and detached in perfect balance.

Balance is not between doing and not doing, but between two positives. It's also the way you do all your positives and the why behind all your positives. It is also not going to either extreme of the positives. For example, when do you detach, for how long do you detach, and why?

Recently, I was watching *America's Got Talent;* there was a lady standing on a tight rope, she balanced a chair on the tight rope. Then she got up on the chair and steadied herself on it. I kept wondering, "What is it that allows her to feel that center point so clearly that she doesn't fall?" For spiritual balance, we have to be so centered to know when to lean in which direction, when it's right to do which thing: actions, silence, detachment, love, tolerance, courage...

We bring about balance by performing actions for the right reasons and being really honest with ourselves. For example, if I use my meditation time to build my spiritual energy, I'm doing it for the right reason. If I use it to escape from action and my life calling, then I'm misusing that solitude. Similarly, I should use the internet to raise myself to a better state or to serve, not to numb myself, or to check out, or simply to frivolously waste time.

I start to get imbalanced when I do things for the wrong reason. For example, I may be a workaholic to feel better about myself or because I'm escaping from something else. Sometimes workaholism is an attempt to fill an empty hole created by a lack of self-worth. In these cases, when an action is not grounded in a pure and positive intention, it will cause imbalance in me. So, how do you do things for the right reason? That's the tricky part. Also, many times the word balance is exploited and used to justify not doing something.

It takes a lot of silence and connection with our core truth to be balanced. If we have a lot of ego or attachment, it's not possible. We have to be free of vices to be balanced. A symptom of balance is a sense of wellbeing, lightness, and clarity. When I'm beginning to practice balance, I ask myself, why am I doing what I'm doing? And when I lose my sense of wellbeing, then I ask myself, in which direction am I going too far?

To master balance, you need a spiritual coach. Otherwise, you can fall off that wire very quickly. Balance is an advanced virtue because you need so much clarity to do it right.

MEDITATION ON
BALANCE

Balance is walking the tightrope of pairs of positive qualities. It is centering between qualities such as enthusiasm and tranquility, between engaging with the world and detaching from the world, between taking time for the self and serving others. For this, we need to experience timeless truths deeply. Cultivating balance brings sustainable happiness into our lives.

Let's begin by sitting in a comfortable position with your hands and feet relaxed and apart. Now find a spot on the wall or the ceiling on which you can focus your attention. It could be a picture or even a candle. Rest your eyes gently on that spot. Now take a deep breath. Breathe in, hold it, and as you exhale relax and clear your mind. Now take another deep comfortable breath, hold it, and exhale. Each time you exhale, this is a signal for your body that it is time to relax.

One...breathe in relaxation and exhale all tension and worry.

Two...take another deep breath and exhale, clearing your mind.

Three...take another deep breath and relax. Notice how relaxed and still you feel.

Mentally take yourself far, far away from your roles and responsibilities. You have all the time in the world, and you are just in the right place. Now, let go of the sounds of the world as you slide into deep silence. Allow the silence to slip inside of you; allow it to permeate your whole being. Allow the self to be here in deep silence for a few moments. You just are.

The only thoughts you have are, "I am. I am stillness itself." Experiencing silence is essential for cultivating balance. Because it brings clarity to the mind and a clear mind is essential for inner equilibrium.

Now, imagine that deep inside you there is a switch that can turn off all the voices in your mind. Turn this switch off now and relax into deep stillness. Allow the noise to disappear as you enter deeply into a state of restful alertness.

Now, take a few moments to remember who you are. You begin to sense that you are peace. In the stillness of your mind, peace unfolds like a warm light into you, the soul. You remember that you are spirit and that before you entered this world, you were complete with peace, with love, with joy. These timeless qualities exist within you forever, and the only reason you lost touch with them is you forget who you are. Take time to remember and experience yourself as light, as peace, as love. Experience of these timeless qualities brings balance into your life.

The more you practice these eternal concepts, the more you experience them, and the more you experience them, the more you can dance on the tightrope of life with ease, lightness, and perfect balance.

Om Shanti – I am Peace.

BENEVOLENCE

Benevolence is the sincere wish to bring true lasting benefit to others because of your love for them. To develop the virtue of benevolence, you must be unselfish, beyond unfair preferences, outside yourself, and beyond your story. This virtue is best summarized in its first two letters, BE. You have to be outside your story and yourself and just be. Then you can bring benefit. Only then can you really be loving towards others and be selfless enough to focus on their good.

Benevolence is an active virtue. In comparison, appreciation occurs more at your thought level. Benevolence starts with a feeling, a feeling of loving concern. That love becomes so strong that it compels you to act for the good of others. You do something to uplift others, to help others, or to support others.

But, it begins with a strong feeling of love and that love compels you to action. You can hold that loving attitude for others, only when you are beyond your self-centered story, and go beyond those limits. Selflessness leads to benevolence. Our benevolence toward others shouldn't depend on their mood or disposition.

MEDITATION ON
BENEVOLENCE

by Bebe Butler (1974 - 2016)

To plant seeds of benevolence means that I plant seeds of pure compassion and love in the world. It means that from my heart I truly want to reach out and uplift the world around me.

True benevolence cannot be contrived; it comes from one place. When the heart is clean, when the mind is quiet, when we can drop our stories and dramas and be in the pure energy of the soul, we will hear two things. One is the sound of peace inside, the sound of the beauty of the world. But the other is the sound of sorrow that exists in the world. Our ability to hear the pain and respond to that pain like a mother would to a crying child, becomes enhanced by silence.

To be benevolent, I have to learn to be silent. Take a moment now and just let everything go. Let your stories go, let the drama go and visualize yourself up on a beautiful mountain, high, high above the world. A place of pristine and pure silence. Where you can feel that great quiet mystery of the world, breathe a silence in until it infuses every cell, every part of your being. Allow the stillness to massage your being until you feel completely relaxed. And now prepare yourself to plant this silence in the world through your mind.

Imagine that above you there is a divine, pure and beautiful light. The Light of the supreme energy and feel this light as it cascades down in the world below you. Feel this light as it pours like a waterfall. Washing away the worries of the world, cleaning every mind, refreshing every heart. Just visualize this healing light, pouring over the entire world. Soothing hearts, soothing fears, healing the elements, nurturing every mind so that the whole world feels a sense of connection. So that the whole world somehow senses they are not alone, but are infinitely connected to an abundant source of light and love.

If I truly want to be benevolent, I have to learn the art of silence and create these small moments where I drop my story and send out peaceful, pure energy to the world around me. I can do this while I am with friends and family. I can do this while I am going about my daily chores and duties. All I have to do is drop my story, be still and send the world the energy of pure peace and love. This practice can do wonders.

Om Shanti – I am Peace.

CAREFREENESS

I heard someone recently say, "Everything real is safe." We can be carefree when we have a deep feeling of trust. When we are in our soul, in our reality, and in connection with the Source, there's a feeling of safety. There's a feeling of support, and there's a feeling that everything is going to be okay in that connection. Because there is safety, you can be carefree. In contrast, when we are caught up in this world where there is no security because the world is always changing. It's unpredictable. Our ultimate feeling of safety and carefreeness comes from knowing that no matter what happens I'm taken care of, I'm supported, and I'm guided. We receive guidance when we are connected to the Source.

That connection gives us a feeling of comfort. It makes us carefree. We feel like a child who's well taken care of. A child doesn't fear that his/her parents might not provide care. When we connect to the Source, we live under a canopy of protection. This, in turn, makes us more and more carefree.

The paradox of being carefree is that you have to care a lot about your spiritual effort to achieve it. You have to take care of your spiritual affairs, your connection to the Source in order to feel that sense of safety and reality. When you're spiritual, you trust that there is benefit in everything. You trust that you're going to be supported spiritually, you know the solutions will come. You trust that you'll always be taken care of on some level and that creates carefreeness.

This is an advanced virtue. The underpinning of carefreeness is trust.

MEDITATION ON
CAREFREENESS

To really be carefree, we have to wake up from the deep slumber of delusion. We have to see through the illusion of the body and the roles we play. We have to understand the deception of seeking sensual pleasures. And, most importantly, we have to awaken to the truth that we are children of the Source. When we open ourselves to the protection and guidance of the Source, then we can truly be carefree.

Let's begin this meditation by traveling far, far away with your mind, away from the world of stories and sounds. You sense yourself getting quieter and quieter as the world of sound disappears. Take a deep breath. As you exhale, the world of sound vanishes and you enter into a sweet, silent communion with yourself the luminous soul and with the Source, the Ocean of Love. Let this beautiful world of silence wash over you like a soft breeze as you absorb the gentle, comforting energy of the Divine, of God. Allow yourself to let go and simply receive whatever God wishes to share with you at this moment.

You sense a sweet presence of love and peace. You feel a heart-to-heart connection with this Supreme luminous light. The first thing God says to you is, "That body made of five elements is not you. It is a costume you are wearing. Just as you take off your costume once your act is over, in much the same way, you will discard your body when your part on this world stage finishes. You, the actor, are never born nor will you ever die. Do not be under the illusion that you are the body."

Take time to reflect on these words. Sense your eternity and remember that you are a soul, the life force of your body.

Again, you feel your heart pulled to the presence of the Ocean of Benevolence. Through the medium of thoughts, you sense God telling you, "You are pure, wise, and flawless. This is your original nature. Step away from the world of illusion that tells you there is scarcity."

You begin to realize that there is a whole spiritual universe. This universe is offering you love, peace, and comfort. When you are in this universe, when you are feeding off this inner world, then no external situation can upset you. You are carefree.

Again, you feel your heart pulled to the presence of the Divine One. God says to you, "You and I are eternally connected. We belong to each other. However you are, whatever you are like, you are mine. You forgot this when you started to identify with the body. Wake up my child from this deep sleep of ignorance. You are eternally pure, wise and flawless. You are mine."

The more you listen to this, the more you realize that you are incorporeal, pure, and spotless, that you are a child of the Supreme Being. You begin to trust that you will always be taken care off. You start to feel carefree because there is a deep knowing that regardless of anything that happens, you will always be guided, you will always be protected.

Om Shanti – I am Peace.

CLARITY

Clarity is where the mind is so uncluttered that we are able to see everything clearly for what it is. With clarity, we don't get deceived or come under negative influences. Clarity is also like discernment; it's the power to distinguish between impulses and desires, wants, and real needs. To make the right choices in life, we need clarity. In fact, to do everything right, we need clarity. If God came to me and said, "You can ask Me for one virtue. I will grant it to you," I would ask for clarity.

With clarity, the soul becomes transparent and pure. When the soul is clear, it can, on its own, discern and do everything correctly. Clarity brings subtlety hence, we always know what is resourceful in each moment.

Someone recently asked me if we can pray to God to take away our financial troubles. I said I'm not sure God is concerned to take away anyone's financial difficulties. I cannot speak for God, of course, I wouldn't know what He/She is thinking at any given moment. But I highly doubt He/She interferes with my or anyone else's financial status. But, God can give me one thing, and that is clarity, and with clarity, I can solve any problem. The only thing I need ask for is clarity because deep down we all have the answers; we all have the solutions and clarity is that underlying virtue that makes solutions possible.

We need a lot of silence and solitude to generate clarity. To regain clarity, we need to practice moving through our day without thinking too much. We shouldn't muddy the waters of our mind with too much analysis, too much thinking, or too much emotion. The mind has to be very still and pure to be clear.

The pure mind is filled with good wishes and pure feelings. It is not overburdened with many desires. The mind needs a clear, simple focal point for it to have clarity. For example, when we choose to practice a virtue, we focus on that specific virtue. We don't think about ten other things, as the mind will tend to do. This is not about trying to blank out the mind completely. That is not possible. The mind will always pick up something to think about. The mind must have a focus. Hence give the mind a virtue or a spiritual concept to focus on. The mind needs to be very still to be clear, and our desires and useless thoughts muddy the mind.

MEDITATION ON
CLARITY

To regain clarity takes a lot of practice. We have to practice clearing the garbage thoughts from our mind, we have to practice filling our heart and mind with only good wishes and pure feelings, and most importantly we have to practice releasing material desires. Decluttering your mind and retraining it becomes easy when you can access wisdom from a Higher Power.

First, let's slow down our breath. Breathe deeply on a count of four and release that breath on the count of 6. Let's repeat this another three times.

Breathe in and release your breath. Breathe in and release your breath. Breathe in and out. Now, imagine a golden light starting from the top of your head and slowly moving down your entire body and coming out through your feet.

Again, visualize a golden light at the top of your head. It is slowly moving through your entire body and coming out through your feet. This time the body is being cleared of any unwanted energies, energies such as laziness and physical pain. It is flushing out negative energies from your body.

Now, your body is supporting you in your meditation. Your head is clear, and your mind has become more receptive. In this state, be a witness to your thoughts. Start by noticing the kinds of thoughts you are having. No judgment; just be a neutral observer of your thoughts.

Again, visualize a golden light at the top of your head. Imagine it descend to the seat of your third eye. This golden light is getting to work on your mind. This time it is flushing out layers of mental and emotional garbage.

Allow the soul to be worked on by the golden light again. This time, it is filling you, the soul, with love and wisdom. You begin to see the spirit, the essence of every person. You experience people on a spiritual level. Everyone is a spiritual being, intrinsically pure and true. With these thoughts, good and pure feelings awaken within you. You send out good wishes and pure feelings to all people across the globe.

You are moving away from differences and begin to feel universal brotherhood toward everyone. This helps you to switch off your internal commentary. In this space, you notice your connection with the Source. You are linked by an eternal thread of love. This contact is helping your mind to settle down. You understand the ripples of waste thoughts in your mind were giving you a distorted vision of yourself and situations. With this relationship and connection with God, the ripples are settling down, and everything is becoming crystal clear.

With this clarity, you begin to notice the thoughts that shape your reality. You also understand the necessity of practice over the long term to retain this clarity. You promise yourself that you will meditate regularly morning and evening.

Om Shanti – I am Peace.

COMPASSION

Compassion is holding love and care for another in my heart and attitude. This feeling moves me to make every effort to alleviate another's suffering. We can only experience this noble sentiment when we are not trapped in our stuff, our story, our head, and when we are willing to listen.

Compassion like benevolence takes a lot of selflessness, because we must be free of any selfish agenda. We must be present to the other. We must understand them and respond with love. We have to be so egoless to be compassionate; it can't be all about me. This is true spirituality. All genuinely spiritual people are compassionate. It is a job requirement.

Even though compassion starts as a pure feeling, it ultimately leads you towards an action that supports people in the world. And it can't come from your ego, or a sense of, "I have so much to give and this poor person... " It is just a pure feeling of love and support for another.

How do we begin to practice compassion? Surprise! It all starts with cleaning our minds. As repetitive as that sounds, most virtues build on each other and compassion builds on cleanliness. Also, reflecting on compassion will give you compassion. All religions, when they are functioning well, aim for compassion because it is a giving virtue. It isn't the only virtue but compassion is a big one because you cannot be a spiritual person without being compassionate.

Pema Chodron once said, "Compassion is not a relationship between the healer and the wounded. It's a relationship between equals." With pure compassion, you're not trying to fix someone or change a situation. You are working collaboratively with a lot of humility to help them find a solution. You are not telling people how they should live their lives; you're just working on giving souls pure energy and support. There's a certain wisdom to deep spiritual compassion. I've noticed my compassion becomes less of a feeling if I get into fixing. When I start wanting to fix someone, I go from feeling love and compassion to let me fix this person. Is there ever a good time and place to give people advice? Yes, if and when they ask for it.

Compassion is also when you become an instrument to create a spiritual safe space for souls to receive love, pure feelings, and support. In this space, you're not having compassion based on their drama; it's just from soul to soul. Also, in this space, there is no attachment. To continually be compassionate, we have to train our mind to regain its strength and share that with others.

MEDITATION ON
COMPASSION

Compassion doesn't differentiate. It doesn't distinguish between race, gender, or nationality. Compassion is the quality that sees behind the labels of the body and understands the need of the soul. The underpinning of compassion is wisdom. It is the wisdom to see that to really meet the long-term needs of all souls; we have to create a spiritual system, a safe space for souls to realize they are pure, flawless, consciousness. The walls of this space are built of good wishes, pure feelings, love, and care.

Visualize you are sitting on a beach watching the waves of the ocean. It is the time just before sunset. The sky is blue with hues of copper and pink. The sand under you feels nice and soft almost like flour. The breeze is blowing the tension right out of your body as you relax listening to the gentle rhythm of the waves.

Imagine the physical world is washed away from your mind with each wave that comes. Your worries go away; your roles go away; your pressures go away. You become aware that you, the soul, are looking out through these eyes onto the ocean waves and beyond to the gorgeous evening sun. This ocean shore is a gateway, a place where you can slip into a safe spiritual world. As the breeze blows over you, you move more and more into this peaceful, spiritual world.

Your mind is clean and free. You are absorbed in being, absorbed in the experience of being the soul sitting in this body looking out through the eyes, observing the beauty of nature and with each wave that comes. You've created a tranquil safe space to be who you truly are—a compassionate, pure, loving, caring, flawless diamond.

Now, with your mind's eye, invite people to come to sit beside you. Invite them to take a sip from these serene waters. Be gentle but firm, understanding that it is not easy for people to step away from the attractions of the physical world, however illusory they are. Keep visualizing their presence in this space. Slowly, they begin to appreciate the pure simplicity of this space. You are kind; you are caring, but firm.

You don't find the need to say anything. Both of you are partaking of the pure stillness of this space. You are beginning to feel restored and refreshed. This naturally draws people to see the beauty you are witnessing, to experience the peace you are relishing. By letting go of the world, the memories, the stresses and cleaning your mind, you have created this compassionate space for others to experience their unique spiritual identity.

Om Shanti – I am Peace.

COURAGE

Courage means I can get up. Every time I fall, I get up. I fall, I get up; I fall, I get up, and that act of getting up is courage. There are two kinds of courage; one is just ego-pride. "I'm great, I can do it; I'm fearless, I'll do this and that." The second kind is courage that comes from the heart, just as the origin of the word tells us (Etymology: from Anglo-French coeur means heart).

When your heart knows what it wants on a deep spiritual level, it's willing to keep getting up and up and up. We see that sometimes parents take amazing risks out of love for their children; or when someone jumps in and saves another out of love. Courage is what compels us to move—a passion for our mission and our vision. A vision of something higher compels us to stand up again because our hearts want a deeper connection with something higher. We have to remind ourselves of this higher emotion to keep standing up. It's the heart that gives us courage to keep going on and on. Without it, if we act just out of ego-pride, it will be tough to have true courage. For example, if one is on a spiritual path for ego, it's hard to keep getting up and up.

To achieve this kind of pure courage, you need a good coach. Having the Source as a Coach increases your courage to do the impossible. For example, consider the Olympians who perform near impossible tasks, after impossible training. And they all have amazing coaches. We all need someone behind us, to encourage us, support us, and inspire us. For real courage on a hero's journey, you need the Source as a Coach.

When we've made contact with our most profound spiritual core, then we have the courage to let go of unwanted actions and feelings. And when we accept that our higher divine self is not separate from us but is that which lies at the very heart of us, then, we receive the strength to keep going. Courage really comes from remembering our highest self and not merely from removing our weaknesses.

I recently watched an interview with Nadia Comaneci (the first person who scored a perfect 10 in gymnastics at the Olympics). The interviewer asked her, "Do you have one piece of advice to give to all the young girls going to the Olympics?" Nadia responded, "Remember your perfect best routine before you go on the floor or the beam."

In summary, there are two places real courage comes from

1. Remembering your highest self.

2. A connection with the Source — it's like being plugged into a power source.

MEDITATION ON
COURAGE

Courage is seeing by the light of the heart. It is taking a step toward something even though it might not be easy because we have faith that God will extend a thousand steps of help. Courage means rebuilding ourselves stronger every time life knocks us down. More than anything else, courage is consistently seeing our highest self and moving forward with that strength.

Let's begin this meditation by taking a few slow and deep breaths. Breathing in, breathing out, and as you allow your breath to slow down, allow your body to slow down, let your mind to slow down. And, again, take a deep breath in and as you exhale allow your relaxation to become twice as deep. Allow yourself to grow twice as relaxed. Again, take a deep breath in and as you exhale go deeper and deeper into that stillness, allowing your body to become completely loose, limp, and relaxed.

Visualize yourself stretched out on a nice patch of grass looking up at a night sky. Allow the earth below you to remove any remaining tension as you become as silent as this beautiful clear sky. The night sky above you is completely still, allow yourself to become like that.

Allow your body to begin to feel weightless. It is as if at this moment you have let go of everything in the world. You have forgotten everything for a few moments as you savor the sweet stillness of the heart. And, it is becoming easier and easier for you to feel this. It is becoming easier and easier for you to sink into this. This stillness is what allows you to open to courage. It allows you to receive from the Higher Source. It is a priceless gift for your life and your strength.

So, again take a deep breath, breathing in slowly and breathing out as you again double your stillness and go even deeper than you could imagine yourself going into this sweet relaxation. And now repeat these sentences in your mind.

1. *I have the courage to face things even when I am afraid.*

2. *I have the courage to look within and discover my true self.*

3. *I have faith that if I take one step of courage, I will receive a thousand steps of help from the Divine Source.*

Go ahead and say these sentences slowly to yourself, feeling them, seeing them, sensing them.

1. *I have the courage to face things even when I am afraid.*

2. *I have the courage to look within and discover my true self.*

3. *I have faith that if I take one step of courage, I will receive a thousand steps of help from the Supreme.*

Remind yourself that deep down you have courage. All you have to do is bring it to the surface with awareness. Let's repeat the sentences.

1. *I have the courage to face things even when I am afraid.*

2. *I have the courage to look within and discover my true self.*

3. *I have faith that if I take one step of courage, I will receive a thousand steps of help from the Supreme.*

Take a moment to feel courage, see courage, and sense courage.

And, now I'm going to invite you to see an image of yourself in your mind. See yourself as courageous. Feel yourself move through life with courage. Take a few moments to visualize what that would look like for you. Imagine what it would feel like in your life, in your mind to have that. Let your imagination go because what you can visualize, you can become.

During the day or before you go to bed, you can do this exercise yourself. Breathing in and breathing out slowly and deeply and saying the three affirmations to yourself.

Now, begin to wiggle your toes, stretch your arms, your legs and prepare now to return to daily life but with courage; with a new sight of you that is centered and courageous.

Om Shanti – I am Peace.

DETERMINATION

Determination is having will power for a higher purpose. To be determined is to keep doing something again and again with firmness while keeping our highest aim in sight. This kind of will power is not sustainable by sheer force alone. It comes from having a very high aim in life, from understanding the value of what you are doing, and why you are doing it. When you know the value and the reason, then you have that impetus to get up and keep going. Determination is a form of discipline. When you keep doing something, you experience the benefit, and then it goes from discipline to a "bliss-cipline." Eventually, it becomes a joy and a source of power. It doesn't tire the soul or cause stress.

The first step in determination might create a little bit of stress because you have to push yourself past inertia. To be able to give yourself the initial push, pick something dear to you. Let's take morning meditation practice as an example; first it may be just sheer will, but after a few weeks you start to understand the value of it, so it becomes easier to apply determination.

Sometimes we just have to stick to a discipline; otherwise, we tend to talk ourselves out of things very quickly. To build determination, you also need a set of non-negotiable disciplines. Let's again take the example of a morning meditation practice. If we decide to do this, some days we might not feel like doing it, but it is essential to at least show-up and do something small. In such situations, ask yourself, what feels nurturing to me right now? Show up for your practice but also listen to yourself. "What feels nurturing? Is it a heart-to-heart conversation?" Or, "Maybe, I need to get up and move" You may not be able to meditate deeply, but you are not letting go of the discipline of meditation.

MEDITATION ON
DETERMINATION

by Bebe Butler (1974 - 2016)

The spiritual journey is a beautiful one. But it is a long journey. I have to travel past the cities and towns of falsehood back home to the light that I truly am. And to embark on this journey, I need a spiritual resolve; I need determination.

There are few things that can help me. Whenever times get challenging, let me remember: "Why is it that I am making this journey?" Take a moment now and ask yourself. "Who is the real me, that I am awakening to?" How do you see yourself after you have traveled past all your challenges and illusions and barriers? Who is the real you beyond all of that?

Take a moment to get clear about your vision. See yourself illuminating that light, that love, that joy. See yourself at the end of the journey. And remind yourself of this every day. Though there will be many times of joy along the journey, there will also be those passages, whether discouragement comes, distraction, storms of temptation or challenging relationships emerge, one thing that can help me keep resolve amidst the storms, is to not give in to the illusions, and that I have to think about the storms. Let me not be impressed by the storms, let me not think, "Why is this happening? What is happening?" But instead, "Let me anchor into that light of who I am," when I focus instead on kindling the awareness of my truth, when I focus instead on nurturing the soul and just let the storm pass.

When I emerge my vision of who I truly am, my resolve increases. Thinking too much about the storm can weaken me and dishearten me. All I have to do is focus on my light. It's that simple. And very soon the journey will become once more illuminated with beauty and I will find myself strengthened. I will find myself wiser having passed through the storm.

But there is one more very important thing I need, to keep my resolve. And that is to pay attention and stay present. There will be many signs and signals along the path. And if I am not paying attention, if I am distracted, I will miss those signs. Just like, if I am daydreaming while traveling on a highway and getting lost, requires that I make more effort. It requires a lot more energy. So, if I stay present, then I will see the signs that point me in the direction of my light. By following those signs and signals, I will stay energized, focused. Let me do these three things, let me keep my vision, let me pass through the storms and let me stay present so that I can reach my destination of pure light.

Om Shanti – I am Peace.

DIGNITY

Dignity comes when we are aware of how divine and precious the soul is. It is the ultimate royalty. Dignity is conduct that values, honors, and respects the true self, whether oneself or others. I respect others as I would want to be respected. I take time to reflect on worthy, noble character traits and act accordingly. My dignity gets compromised when I stay in situations that don't make me feel valued and honored.

We pay mightily for our lack of dignity. We pay by losing our sense of self-worth, which in turn erodes the very fabric of the soul. Especially when we are insecure, and in codependent relationships, we lose our sense of self and dignity because we give in to the temptation of being cowardly and forget to nurture the soul as an independent precious being, worthy of pure love.

I have to take great care to protect the dignity of others as I would protect my own. I preserve my own dignity by protecting my principles. Dignity is one of the most important virtues. When you compromise your dignity, you fall into a downward spiral that leads you to disrespect and eventually dislike yourself.

Ultimately dignity comes when we deeply understand that our worth comes from a divine Source and so is not something we merely wish or imagine for ourselves. It manifests when we are in soul space and act from that spiritual position. In dignity, we realize that we are precious, and that other people are precious—this is high divinity.

MEDITATION ON
DIGNITY

Dignity comes from deep inside the spirit. It is when the spirit is filled with nobility and possesses an attitude of honor towards the self and others. It happens when we learn to value our own heart and mind and tend to them with love and care. Dignity is also treating others with respect as I would want to be treated.

Most importantly, you can't chase after dignity; it naturally follows you if you live by high principles. The opposite of dignity is codependency. When our minds are caged by over-identifying with bodies and physical relationships, then we lose our dignity. To move into a state of inner dignity, let's learn the art of treating our minds and hearts as sacred places.

Start by imagining your ideal meditation room overlooking a seashore. This room is pristine clean, with gorgeous wooden floors, big windows, and sparsely furnished. You have a comfortable seat for your meditation. Take that seat. Now gently but firmly, let go of stories and dramas. Push them out of the window onto the sea, just be in the spirit for a few moments. The true spirit has no story, no drama; it is simply pure vibration.

You feel completely still and peaceful in this meditation room. For the next few moments, you can sanctify your mind. Take this moment to empty the contents of your mind and imagine them disappearing into the sea. If I want dignity, then I have to learn the art of filling my mind with only sacred thoughts, with thoughts of peace, wisdom, and contentment.

Now think of the quality of contentment. Allow that quality to fill your being completely. And, just allow yourself to be, allow yourself to be satisfied with everything and everyone. You feel content just to exist in this pure vibration of sacred silence.

Now take this moment to empty the negative and wasteful contents of your heart. If you want to live in dignity, then you have to let go of mucky feelings coursing through your heart. We have to fill our heart with only feelings of benevolence and beauty. Now, open your heart to the ocean of pure energy that is always flowing toward you. In this sacred stillness, you sense the ocean of divine energy flowing through the universe. You allow it to fill every fiber of your being. You sense your heart becoming pure and strong.

In this gorgeous meditation room overlooking the sea, with your mind healthy, and your heart strong, you revisit your highest principles. Take this moment to remind yourself of the three principles you value most. Repeat these principles in your mind. Go ahead and say these principles slowly to yourself, feeling them seeing them, sensing them.

And, now I'm going to invite you to see an image of yourself in your mind. See yourself as calm and dignified. You are moving through your life with calmness and nobility. Take a few moments to visualize what that would look like for you. Imagine what it would feel like in your body, in your mind to have that. Let your imagination go, because what you can visualize, you can become.

We receive the special gift of dignity when we learn to engage with the world while living in our highest truth. With this simple practice of learning to fill your mind with sacred thoughts and fill your heart with the divine, pure energy of the universe, dignity becomes your natural nature.

Om Shanti – I am Peace.

FORGIVENESS

In order to forgive, remember you are starring in a grand epic movie going on around you. See it as the most magnificent production in movie history. The whole world is a stage (as Shakespeare said), and all of the more than 7 billion people on Earth are acting in this grand epic movie. Your role and other people's roles say nothing about who you, the soul, are personally. Just like in a movie, no good or evil in the movie affects the actors outside of the movie. You, the soul, are merely acting in this grand epic movie, this drama. Therefore, you can forgive.

To easily forgive, you can also look at life as a dream. When you wake up from a bad dream, you don't lament, "I had this bad dream, and those people did a terrible thing to me." No, you understand that it was a dream and so you are not upset with them. The trick is to wake up spiritually. This paves the way for deep forgiveness. When we realize our world is just like a movie or a dream and doesn't affect us, then we can easily absolve ourselves and others.

There is superficial forgiveness, when we say this person's doing the best they can, or that they are God's children. Or, we try to understand what they are going through. But for sincere, lasting forgiveness, we need to be aware that, "all the world's a stage and all men and women merely players..."

When we think the movie is real life, we hold grudges toward other people. We must find our meaning in a deep place of the soul, in connection with the Source. Only then can we feel that mercy and love for other souls.

Forgiveness helps the forgiver more than the "forgivee." When we refuse to forgive, we hold poison in our hearts. This poison hurts us more than the one we refuse to forgive. Therefore, forgive, forgive, forgive! Do whatever it takes to forgive, because if you don't, this will hinder your spiritual progress more than anything else. Holding bitterness inside your heart harms you the most. It's like a festering wound that doesn't just go away because you are ignoring it. This wound poisons your whole being; it poisons everything around you—your relationships, your peace of mind, and your outlook on life.

Another essential aspect of forgiveness is forgiving the self and not feeling guilty. After the movie is over, the actors have a wrap party and go home. They don't blame each other for what they did on stage. So, in our lives, if we are sick or something happened to us in my childhood, and we keep lamenting, "What did I do to deserve this?" then, we're not acting as a witness to our movie. This makes it hard to forgive ourselves. For me, the profound realization is - none of this means anything. We can't forgive if we consider the drama we are starring in as real.

For example, Meryl Streep in *Get Ready for Ricki* plays an irresponsible, crazy mom. Whatever happens in that movie doesn't mean anything about Meryl Streep. She is Meryl Streep, and the movie is just a movie. Remembering this wakes us up from the dream.

MEDITATION ON
FORGIVENESS

by Bebe Butler (1974 - 2016)

There is a space inside my being that is known as the heart. And when I have pure feelings for the people in my heart, when I have love and openness towards others, the heart is a place of illumination. When the heart is filled with truth and with pure feelings, I feel a sense of joy, of lightness in life and its if I have no burdens. I am able to be carefree. But when I hold any type of grudge or resentment, that resentment becomes a cage that keeps me from my own goodness.

Allow yourself to move into a space of stillness. As you prepare to reflect on a question, think of one person in your life for whom you hold resentment. Someone that you can't forgive and ask yourself, how do you see this person in your mind? When you interact with them when you talk to them when you think about them. How do you see them in your mind? Chances are, you see their defects, you see their weaknesses, and you continually see the mistakes they have made and that vision becomes a prison.

Now moving back into that space of reflection, ask yourself, is that absolutely who that person truly is? Is that absolutely who that person truly is? Or Is that perception of them, a cage that holds both of us. To release yourself from resentment, understanding is essential and most importantly the understanding of our universal story. So, take a deep breath and allow yourself to go on a journey, beyond the limits of your perception beyond time and into the eternal story of the soul. Let go of the world that holds you and enter in, to a different space.

As souls, we come from a region of light, pure silence, where there is no sound, where there is no time. So just sense yourself there. This is where every single one of us come from; this is the home of souls, beyond physicality, an ocean of light, an ocean of peace. Allow yourself to be immersed in that ocean of peace, as you remember the true nature of all living beings around you.

All of us come from that world, and we enter the physical dimension. We enter this world to play our parts in the stage of the earth, to experience life in the physical form. And when we first begin the path is filled with joy, it's illuminated with the qualities of our souls. But something happens, after many births and after much time has passed, we go from a place of innocence and freedom and truth and soulfulness, and we journey on to a place where we feel more and more distant from our souls. It is as if we develop spiritual amnesia. We get caught in the physical and all of a sudden, we experience loneliness. We experience separation from our soul and from God, and it's as if, all souls become like orphans lost and in pain. It is only from this pain that all of us have caused each other sorrow. When we have pain, we can only give pain. But it's not our natural nature.

If I want to change the vision of the person that I resent or can't forgive, I have to let go of that small vision, that cage I hold them in. And remember our universal story, that we are all doing our best and the only pain came from being separated from our own light. When I can remember this, I can begin to shift my mind to a place of understanding, and I can begin to see other souls, as God sees them. And instead of demanding them to be a certain way, I can love them for who they truly are. Who they have forgotten themselves to be. In this way, I will step out of the cage of resentment and return to that beautiful space of the heart, that is illuminated, that is light, that is beautiful. When you are able to do this, you will once more travel the journey of life back home to your real self and to your natural state of joy.

FREEDOM

Janice Joplin sang it best, "Freedom's just another word for nothin' left to lose." In a state of freedom, you have no fear of losing anything in this world - reputation, physical comfort, wealth, or power. When you are so fixed in the soul that you feel you've got nothing you can lose, and even if something is apparently lost, you'll be okay—that is freedom. You are independent. You are not taking your self-worth and your security from external transitory things. You are really free when your sense of self-worth and identity do not come from how much respect people give you, how many toys you have in the world, or how much money you possess.

Like a bird that flies in the sky, you can land on the branches, but you are not stuck in the world. The trappings of the world are not some tight garments wrapped around you. You just come and go, and you know that you have nothing to lose because you find everything in the spirit.

True freedom is an advanced virtue, and we can achieve it. Everyone wants freedom, but most are not willing to do the work that it requires. Birds sometimes feel trapped in a cage when its door is wide open. Similarly, people are not willing to step out of the cage because they refuse to "see" the exit. Sometimes we mistakenly think that freedom is to move away from everything; but real freedom comes from moving into the spirit. Most bondage these days is psychological. Therefore, mentally with our minds, we move away from the traps and fly freely toward enlightenment.

MEDITATION ON
FREEDOM

Freedom's just another word for the stillness of a self-realized soul.

To be free, we can't be trapped in the cage of name, regard, body, or comfort. When you feel like you've got nothing to lose, when you are so absorbed in the stillness of the soul, and when your sense of self-worth and identity do not come from the respect people give you, or how many toys you have, or how much money you possess—that's when you have real freedom.

There is a science to spiritual freedom. You have to trust in silence as much as you trust in science. With patience and compassion turn inward and talk to yourself, "I'm an eternal being and the real me, the soul, is connected with the Supreme." When you experience these timeless truths, of your true identity, of your eternal relationship with the Source, then you begin to feel free.

Imagine a beautiful bird in flight. You watch the bird soar. You understand that to soar like this bird; you can't derive your sense of worth and security from external transitory things. Again, watch the bird soar. You become one with the bird. You, the soul, are flying, flying free. You are boundless. You are independent. You soar and dip, soar and dip like a free bird. You gracefully land on a tree branch.

You remember that freedom is not to move away from everything, but rather to move into the spirit, into your beautiful enduring pure qualities. You become still and connect with the peace and joy that is deep inside you. You discover that this is the real you... You go beyond wanting respect or possessions or money.. You let them all go. As you let go, you begin to fly again. You soar again. You soar and dip, soar and dip.

You gently swoop down and land on a branch, but you don't attach yourself to it. You are not stuck in the world. The trappings of the world cannot cage you. You can fly and land as you wish. You just come and go, knowing that you really have nothing to lose because everything exists in spirit. You are unbound. You are ecstatic. You are free.

Om Shanti – I am Peace.

GENTLENESS

In gentleness, I stay close to my real feeling of myself. I'm quiet. I'm sensitive to the being of others. I never hurt someone's feelings due to being out of touch with my own. I don't force, or push, or try to change things. Gentleness is the cornerstone of a spiritual person. There's humility in gentleness that doesn't judge. A humility that doesn't force people, doesn't interfere, accepts them as they are, is sensitive to where they are, and to what's going on in their minds. It's a quality that has a lot of respect for others, especially for other people's personal space, and other people's choices.

A gentle person has enough wisdom to know that the story is deeper than they can fathom or imagine. There's just a quiet presence that gives people the feeling of acceptance, of being nurtured. It's like a gentle breeze. It's soothing. It's calming. Their presence is calming because it's not trying to change or fix anything. It's just in its own light and sensitively connecting to others. It brings up the innocence in people. When you see true gentleness, as in a little kitten, or a baby, then their innocence emerges our innocence. And, yet there's wisdom in it.

Only with wisdom is it possible to be gentle. Gentleness also requires some mental balancing. It requires us to perform some metaphysical tight rope walking because we need to know when to get back into our own space, plug into our feelings, and plug into other people's feelings about things, and then operate from that space. Gentleness comes when there is wisdom and humility.

MEDITATION ON
GENTLENESS

by Bebe Butler (1974 - 2016)

Sometimes we have a tendency to punish ourselves, for the mistakes we have made, for the weaknesses we can't seem to overcome. This is an invitation to let go of that tendency. In order to learn how to be gentle with myself, I have to tell myself the right story about the situation I am in. Gentleness is not just kindness, but real deep gentleness can come only when there is wisdom.

Take a moment now to breathe, to relax, to send to yourself and move into that still silent space in the mind. And prepare yourself to go on a journey. Right now leave the world of right and wrong and good and bad and judgement. Leave that world behind along with any memories, as you keep punishing yourself for. Just let it go in a second.

As you wander into a field of spirituality with air fragrant with peace, where there is a quiet joy in the air, a field beyond right and wrong, a sanctuary for your soul and allow yourself to lie there in the grass and let the gentle beauty blow right through you like a fresh breeze. Soothing your mind, blowing away the harsh feelings you have for yourself. In this field beyond right and wrong, it is easy to understand that even your mistakes and your weaknesses are good because they are part of your trail towards wisdom. And the best thing you could learn is just how to grow from them. And your mistakes have also possibly been part of other people's trails towards wisdom. In this field of spirituality, even the imperfect is perfect. It's designed to empower you and awaken you and is only painful when we don't see it that way.

Look at the gentleness of the clouds moving softly across the sky. And allow that softness to move through you, as you realize, that all is well. In the space of the soul, there is only learning and only experience. And we can only do our best, that's it. By punishing ourselves, we only delay the wisdom. So allow the soft, gentle vibrations of this field to help you see the beauty in the imperfection of your mistakes. Can you see what you have learned from them? Can you see how they have also taught other people things? Gentleness sees the beauty in imperfection. And it understands that sometimes transformation is only possible through those experiences.

Take another slow deep breath and prepare to leave this beautiful, gentle field, beyond right and wrong. But carry your gentleness with you. Carry the wisdom of a new story back with you to that world. Knowing you don't have to punish yourself any longer. See yourself in the world moving with gentleness and moving with a wisdom that comes from understanding. Even the most difficult mistakes and weaknesses are part of our trail towards beauty and wisdom.

Om Shanti – I am Peace.

HARMONY

Harmony is linked to lightness. I feel most in harmony when I'm light, and I don't have a burden in my heart. When my mind is light, I flow with people, love people, and work with them. When I'm tense or holding something in my heart, I don't feel light inside, nor clean. Hence it is harder to be in harmony.

The other thing about harmony is that we have to accept we are not always right. If we operate with this feeling, that we are always right, then definitely there is no harmony. If we always insist on our own opinion of something and think we know best, we are correct, and things must be done our way, then harmony isn't possible. It requires an intention to cooperate with others, instead of proving ourselves right.

Being in harmony is analogous to an orchestra in which all the wind instruments, the string, percussion, and bass instruments all play in harmony to create beautiful music. Each section of the orchestra and each musician has his or her part in the music. Similarly, knowing your role in a team, or relationship, helps tremendously in creating harmony. What is your contribution? What is your role? When do you step in and when do you just let things be? Understanding this enables me to be a team player and harmonize. Instead of playing my part, if I judge others, assuming I know best what they should do, then I create discord.

If I'm supposed to play the trumpet, but I'm focused on and judging the person playing the cello, then I create cacophony both in my head and within the group. When I know, what I can do well, and I bring that to the table then I help to create harmony. This harmony brings unity. I know what my talent is, I know what I have to offer, and I don't judge what others are doing. I do what I need to do, and I don't assume I know exactly how best to do someone else's job.

My role is to engage my talents as beautifully as possible to add to the dynamic harmony. That will bring unity. I've also noticed that we harmonize when we are free of stress. When we are light, when the mind is clean, we carry no grudge or burden

MEDITATION ON
HARMONY

Just as a river boldly flows no matter what the obstacle, a harmonious person is always flowing moving forward, not getting stuck in conflicts with anyone. Just as a river is steady, welcoming, and refreshing being in harmony means to flow with people, to work with people, to love people and to be light about it all. When the mind is light, two things happen. First comes the tendency to unite people, secondly the quality of harmony grows inside.

Let's begin this meditation by imagining that you are in a robust ecosystem. There is a beautiful river flowing; there are mighty trees rooted in the fertile soil on either side of the river. There is a community of flora and fauna around you. You are amidst a delicate but hardy cycle of life.

Breathe in the fresh air, and slowly release that breath. Take a few more slow and deep breaths. Breathing in, breathing out and as you allow your breath to slow down, allow your body to become one with the habitat around you, allow your mind to come into harmony with nature.

Your mind is beginning to feel as fresh and clean as the air you are breathing. Again, take a deep breath in and as you exhale allow your mind to become still and light. Breathing in and breathing out slowly and deeply say to yourself, "I am still, calm, relaxed. I am light." "I am, still, calm, relaxed. I am light."

In this stillness, you begin to see your gifts. It opens your heart, and you can access your unique contribution to the world. This stillness is so much more than just quietness; it opens you up to intuition. It gives you the strength to accept your gift and not be afraid of it.

Now, I invite you to see your unique gift, your special contribution. See yourself embodying the gift. See yourself moving through life using the gift. Take a few moments to visualize what that would look like for you. How does it feel to possess this gift? Sense it and see yourself using this gift to benefit others. Let your imagination go because what you can visualize, you can become.

Now, take a deep breath in and as you exhale go deeper and deeper back into that stillness, allowing your body to become completely relaxed. Savor the fresh breeze, the delicate ecosystem, allow yourself to feel privileged to be part of this cycle of life. Watch how the river is flowing purposefully but harmoniously toward its destination. The river is whispering its wisdom to you, the wisdom that you were born to be united, to flow with people, and to be harmonious in your little human ecosystem.

And now repeat these words in your mind. "I flow, create peace, and bring harmony." "I flow, create peace, and bring harmony." "I flow, create peace, and bring harmony."

Slowly begin to stretch. Stretch your arms, your legs and prepare now to return to daily life but with tranquility, with a new sight into your unique gifts, and ready to be harmonious, and ready to enjoy your life.

Om Shanti – I am Peace.

HUMILITY

Think about a person who knows his or her spiritual beauty. How would that person feel? Such a person would feel luminous, precious, and connected to the Source. This one would feel successful and happy not because of anything going on in the drama around him/her, but rather because this one sees his or her inner beauty clearly. People who are like this also see that beauty in other people. A humble person makes others feel special in their presence. That presence puts people in touch with their goodness. A humble person doesn't try to draw attention to himself or herself but is always giving attention to others and uplifting them.

Ultimately, humility is to share our high vision with others. Everyone is capable of higher consciousness. Everyone has that inner beauty. In humility, you not only see it in yourself but also in others. If you experience true humility, you will see beauty in everyone around you, for everyone possesses that same purity within.

Sometimes people mistake humility for the feeling of, "I'm no good," or "Someone is so much better than me," or, "I'm unworthy to be with someone." Real humility is when you value your true inner self no more or no less than the true self of others. You know and understand your capacity, and you are unpretentious about it. A humble person steps away from his or her feelings and opinions and genuinely listens to the experiences of another human being. Your ability to hold people in your heart and care about them adds to your humility.

In humility, we know that we are working on behalf of the Source. We are stewards or instruments for this higher Being or purpose. Any person who creates something of profound significance, something that touches people's hearts and changes lives, knows that they did not act alone. Something higher worked through them. When I have this awareness that something is working through me, that is when I'm truly humble. Deep humility is not possible unless we know that we are instruments of a greater reality. And, we can only have this consciousness when we see that God is working through us. God will only work through us if we sustain a certain level of purity, selflessness, and humility.

Humility is a truly advanced virtue. It requires that we not draw attention to ourselves. We are not wrapped up in a body conscious view of the world. Our spiritual vision and our God-given gifts are so much in our awareness that we do not get caught up in any mundane vision. We do not worry about how others perceive us; what people will think if we do this or that. We do not act to get attention—this my dear friends is humility.

MEDITATION ON
HUMILITY

by Bebe Butler (1974 - 2016)

It is easy to be humble when I play it small. But we are not living in this time to play small; we are living in these times to discover our own greatness. Each one of us carries gifts within us; we are brilliant, divine, radiant and gifted beings. And, our role in these times is merely to cultivate and express those gifts. Whether it's the gift of music, whether it's the gift of loving others, whether it's the gift of being able to give others a sense of peace, or being able to express myself through writing. My job is to cultivate the gift. But then how do I keep my humility as the greatness within awakens?

One of the first steps is that I become aware that when I use my gifts for humanity, there is always a feeling that divine energy is flowing through me, giving me more power than I would ever have on my own. Humility can come when I have the awareness that I am an instrument of the Divine, and this gift is a gift from the Divine.

Humility can come when I realize that I am not the only one that has this special gift within me, but every one of us is magical and radiant and full of beautiful gifts to share with humanity.

I can also cultivate humility by letting go of my attachment to outcomes. Let me allow the Divine to use the gifts, let me let go of my ideas of how I want my gifts to be used or how I want people to accept them or like them. Let me let go of peoples' opinions. I don't have to have a plan of how to put that gift out there. My role is simply to connect with my soul, express the gifts and surrender them to the divine energy of the universe knowing that this gift is not mine. It is one that is destined to be used for the upliftment of humanity.

With humility, I am not attached to success or failure, appreciation or rejection. I just enjoy the joy I find from pure expression of the magic that is within me, and I let go and recognize that the magic is coming from a Supreme Source. All I have to do is to let it flow; all I have to do is tend to my gifts daily and use them daily, and my destiny will unfold naturally. I will find my own way to connect with the world in a meaningful way. I will discover the greatness, the magic within me, but also within every other living being on this earth. With humility, I can express these gifts of easiness, detachment, love, joy, and spirit of service.

Om Shanti – I am Peace.

INNOCENCE

When I reflect on the innocence in a child, I observe that they see through the eyes of wonder. For innocent children, everything is new, and everything is fresh. They are not jaded. They do not live in a world of judgment. They live in a world of awe, openness, and presence. We embody innocence when our perceptions arise from that awe, that mystery and spiritual vision. Innocence is our ability to see beauty. It is our ability not to get trapped in jaded histories, old visions of people, old opinions, and judgments. The virtue of innocence brings a refreshing presence, a simplicity and openness, to each moment.

To be innocent even as an adult, I must be free from vices. My mind should be as innocent as a newborn child and as wise as an experienced sage. I must let go of cynicism and appreciate the simple things in life. The opposite of innocence is cynicism. Cynicism hurts the fabric of humanity. Our collective cynicism is what ails a lot of humanity these days. Actually, many people are proud of their cynicism.

Cynical people are jaded and bitter about the world. Whereas, people who have a sage-like innocence see the beauty and wonder in simple things, in moments, in exchanges. They bring "presence" to everything. If we are jaded or bitter about the world, then we are holding on to an old story, an old opinion. We are stuck; we are unable to move on to the next moment. Innocence is fresh. Cynicism is like muddy water that just sits there and stagnates. Cynical people have old perceptions and opinions that sit and fester day after day, and which they carry into every moment.

Innocence requires us to let go of the past, to keep letting go of the past, and to continually arrive at the present with new eyes. This kind of innocence is not revered in today's culture, because people don't have eyes to see its value. In today's culture, people are often valued for their harsh judgments, and even for their cynicism. People look at innocence as a weakness, a sign that one is naïve, and does not grasp the world.

To be innocent, we must let go of cynical worldly views. The innocent doesn't care what people think or value, because they know their own true value. Innocence is original. When you look at the expressions of children, they are so out of the box. They are not stuck in any "have to's," "shoulds," or conventions. They are uniquely themselves. They arrive at each moment with unique perceptions, ideas, and expressions.

MEDITATION ON
INNOCENCE

All human beings have a space inside that is filled with innocence. When a soul begins its life, that space is completely flawless, filled with light, laughter, and love. Now, for some that space is a squalid shack, for some an abandoned abode, for some a filthy fortress, and for some it is a pillaged palace, somewhere in their soul. Every time we knowingly or unknowingly allow our inner space to be occupied by external influences, we lose some of that innocence.

With this meditation, let's return to our sweet home, our innocence—a home where laughter happens and where you can be vulnerable: a space when you step inside, you'll feel sweetness and wonder; mystery and magic, and where you can express what is sacred to you with originality and presence.

Take a few slow deep breaths. Breathing in, breathing out and as you allow your breath to slow down, allow your body to slow down, allow your mind to slow down. Visualize yourself stretched out on a comfortable bed in a room in a beautiful palace high upon a hill overlooking luscious gardens. Again, take a deep breath in and as you exhale allow your relaxation to become twice as deep. As you breathe in and out, mentally step away from your story, your beliefs, your dramas. Just for a few moments empty your soul of these things.

As you allow your breath to move fluidly in and out, the room you are in is filling with light and becoming absolutely still. It is a beautiful sanctuary of light. In this space, you can feel your purity and innocence. It is like nothing has ever happened to you. Your mind is open and carefree, simple, quiet, easy and you feel connected to the flawless soul within.

At this moment ask yourself the question, who would you be, if nothing had ever happened to you. Who would you be? Feel that sense of freedom, that sense of cleanliness. Allow yourself to take rest from the story of you as you enjoy the pristine nature of the original self.

With your mind's eye take a walk around the beautiful palace with that feeling of lightness and ease. Observe the beauty of the space. You know somewhere deep inside that the beauty you see outside is also your beauty.

Now, take a stroll in the luscious gardens as you breathe deeply in and out. As you observe the beauty of the flowers, the fresh air, the still sky, your mind is becoming clearer and cleaner. For a few moments, enjoy this exquisite space within you that is untouched by the world.

Now, slowly come back to the bedroom and lay down on the bed. Again, take a deep breath in and as you exhale allow your body to become weightless. Here in the sanctuary, you are a pure, innocent being of light. Take a few moments to visualize what that would look like for you. Imagine what it would feel like in your mind to be that. Enjoy this pure space of being beyond all stories untouched by the world. Appreciate your innocence, own your innocence.

Now, begin to wiggle your toes, stretch your arms, your legs and prepare now to return to daily life but with a new perceptive, with awe, with mystery, with lightness, and with a pure spiritual vision of yourself.

Om Shanti – I am Peace.

RESPONSIBILITY

Responsibility is an adult virtue. Children don't necessarily feel responsible. This is especially true of spiritually immature people. Responsibility comes when we understand our unique offering to the whole and make that offering, i.e., do our duty. If I think I don't have anything to offer, then I won't feel responsible. To act responsibly, you need to have faith in your talents, in your gifts, and how those talents and gifts make an essential contribution to the whole. For example, in a gourmet dish, salt is as essential as the other ingredients. Even without an apparently minor ingredient like salt, the dish may not be very tasty.

Similarly, your gifts might not seem very important to you; they might feel similar to salt in a gourmet dish. But, when you understand your gift is valuable, then you'll feel responsible. You will do what is required, and you will feel answerable.

Responsibility is a thread that runs throughout all the virtues. The more we are responsible for developing our virtues and gifting them to others, the stronger all the virtues become in us. As you develop the other virtues and take them seriously, you will naturally spread those virtues to others. Virtue is the greatest fortune; we should try to help others so that everyone can enjoy this fortune. This is what it means to be responsible.

In today's culture, we talk endlessly about rights. However, the conversation is not complete until we also talk about our responsibilities. To sustain our rights, we must address our responsibilities. We need to understand the responsibilities we have in order to claim our rights. We need to understand two things here. First, how are we using our rights? Are we using them to become better persons? This is responsibility to the self. Second, we also have a responsibility to society, to people. We shouldn't just talk about what is owed to us, but also what we owe to the community.

Responsibility is also the willingness to respond to what's in your power to change for the better. We must first discern what is it that we have the power to change. We must first exercise our power over our thoughts and gifts. We can change the world by doing the things that are within our capacity.

Responsibility comes from realizing that there are things we can change, and there are ways we can respond, through our thoughts, through our actions, and our gifts. Our life is a responsible response to a need for change. We don't neglect what's in front of us. Responsibility is the ability to respond, it is the ability to care, and to take care of what needs to be taken care of. Responsibility empowers us to uplift and be uplifted.

MEDITATION ON
RESPONSIBILITY

Responsibility is about caring; it's about compassion. It is the virtue of honor threaded into our relationships. There is something about responsibility that connects us to all other souls. Responsibility is one of those virtues that pays it forward. When you do something good for people, then everyone who benefits will be inspired to do it also. This is the kind of world we want where everyone uses their rights and responsibilities to help others. Those people who are helped will then become the next helpers.

Let's take this opportunity to help others. Begin this meditation by taking a few slow and deep breaths. Breathing in, breathing out and as you allow your breath to slow down, allow your body to slow down, allow your mind to slow down. And, again, take a deep breath in and as you exhale allow your relaxation to become twice as deep. Allow yourself to become twice as relaxed. Again, take a deep breath in and as you exhale go deeper and deeper into that stillness, allowing your body to become completely lose and limp and relaxed.

It is as if at this moment you have let go of everything of the world. You have forgotten everything for a few moments as you savor the sweet stillness of the heart. And, it is becoming easier and easier for you to feel this. It is becoming easier and easier for you to sink into this. This stillness is what allows you to open to experiencing your gifts. It shows you how fortunate you are. It is a priceless tool for your life.

So, again take a deep breath, breathing in slowly and breathing out as you again double your stillness and go even deeper than you could imagine yourself going into this sweet relaxation. And now repeat these words in your mind. "I am eternal light and goodness." "My real nature is beautiful, caring, and compassionate." "I am supremely fortunate." Go ahead and say these sentences slowly to yourself.

Again, "I am eternal light and goodness. My real nature is beautiful, caring, and compassionate. I am supremely fortunate."

Again, feeling them seeing them, sensing them. "I am eternal light and goodness. My real nature is beautiful and generous. I am supremely fortunate."

And, now I'm going to invite you to see an image of yourself in your mind. See yourself as a responsible, fortunate person. See yourself moving through your life with deep knowing that you are extremely fortunate and that you have a responsibility to share that fortune. Take a few moments to visualize what that would look like for you. This is your true personality. Imagine what it would feel like to fulfill your true responsibility to be natural, real, and caring. Take a moment now and value your gifts, value your fortune.

Breathe in and out slowly and deeply and relax back into stillness. In this stillness, you can look inside and discover the fortune you already have. It gives you the strength to accept that you already are everything you could ever dream of becoming. You are supremely fortunate. In this state, you feel open to fulfilling your responsibilities. You begin to understand and accept that spreading your virtue and good fortune to everyone is your real responsibility.

Slowly but gently return to daily life but with generosity, with calm, and with new insights on your real and natural nature.

Om Shanti – I am Peace.

SELF-RESPECT

Self-respect is to possess deep love and regard for the self. I focus on my inner beauty and treat myself as I would a dear friend. Real self-respect is very different from pride. A proud or vain person tweets a show to the world, but to really, deeply respect ourselves we have to align our thinking and doing to our highest principles. We have to live in integrity. We have to be responsible. Self-respect comes from being in touch with the innate purity of the soul. As a self-respecting soul, I am completely in touch with myself as a soul. There is no taking or grabbing for material things. I do not take my feeling of self-worth from external things. In self-respect, I live beyond labels of gender, color, race, position. I don't depend upon my ego image.

Self-respect comes from giving of myself to others – my time, my resources. One cannot have self-respect without being generous. My life has to be for a higher purpose, for a higher cause. Mere ambition for physical, temporary attainments will not give me self-respect. Material success might make us proud, but it will not give us self-respect. Self-respect comes from using our talents for a higher cause, for a higher purpose.

You can do all the right things, but if you don't have a deep connection with yourself, there is no deep self-respect. Self-respect is knowing my worth beyond the world of action. It's having a profound sense of yourself beyond the world of form and doing. Self-respect comes from a deep experience of our own light, our own divinity, our own awareness as spiritual beings in the world of form. With this understanding, we perform righteous actions in the world and are also detached from the world.

MEDITATION ON
SELF-RESPECT

by Bebe Butler (1974 - 2016)

I prepare to meditate on respect. And there are many types of respect. I can respect the natural world around me, I can respect other people, but for right now, I am going to focus on respecting myself. At the core of any type of respect is a vision of love. When I truly respect something, I care about it deeply, and at the depths of this care, there is the feeling that what I care for is absolutely precious and valuable.

Too often I think of myself as just a mundane physical being, and I think only of my external world. But I take a few moments to go inside myself and sense the spirit, the essence of peace within my physical body. This soul dwells in the center of the forehead, and I relax and let go, into a stillness that is untouched, by anything of the external world.

In my mind, I travel beyond the physical, to a dimension of silence, a place beyond even the sound of a thought, where it is truly as if I am bathing in the light of peace. This is the home of the soul. When I take my mind here, I can let go of the external and experience the precious beauty of my internal world. I let go into that peace. And I allow waves of this still light to bathe my entire being. In this peace, it's easy to see that I am only an actor playing roles. I take many costumes and bodies, and I travel to the physical dimension, but my true nature is a soul, a spark of light.

I am a traveler through time. And within me are enormous powers that I have forgotten - the power to love, the power to transform my external environments with pure thoughts. I am an enormously powerful being of light, a child of the Supreme Being. When I remember how precious I truly am, and I can carry this awareness in the physical world and instead of being a mundane world, the world becomes a magical place to live. This respect for myself changes my interaction with nature and the world around me. To truly respect myself and anything else, I only need to develop the eyes to see how precious I truly am.

Om Shanti – I am Peace.

SELF-SOVEREIGNTY

When I think of this virtue, the wise old sovereigns of fairy tales come to mind. In many of these stories, everyone would bow and listen to what the good old kings said. One who is a self-sovereign has such benevolence and is a natural leader. Others naturally want to follow them in action and thought. A self-sovereign has command over their thoughts and emotions. Their view of situations and people is filled with love and benevolence. Because of these qualities, they are good rulers and leaders.

A self-sovereign has a wealth of virtues, talents, and spiritual experiences. Because of this spiritual wealth, persons with self-sovereignty wouldn't have any external desires. They do not beg for anything from anyone, nor do they have any desire to manipulate or exploit others because they are so rich with experiences, virtues, and powers. When you have everything you can imagine on the soul level, then you never ask for anything. And because you have no selfish desires, you can be trusted.

A self-sovereign is a master over the senses. For example, one doesn't over-eat, or comfort-eat or get pulled by sugar or alcohol. There is complete control over eyes, tongue, and sense of smell. One's inner kingdom is completely under one's command.

Someone recently said, "If you want to find the most powerful person in the room, look for the calmest person in the room. The one whose breathing is the slowest. The one who's sitting the most still." People who are self-sovereign are so centered in their fullness that they are not running in a million directions chasing after taste, sounds, sights, fame, or wealth. A self-sovereign is internally full and wealthy, and so lacks nothing.

MEDITATION ON
SELF-SOVEREIGNTY

Self-sovereignty has very little to do with ruling over people; it is having command over the self. It is mastery over the senses, mastery over our mind, mastery over our attitudes. It is about ruling one's own heart and mind with compassion. Self-sovereignty means being steady in an inner state of dignity.

Watch your breath as it flows in and out. It is fluidly flowing in and out, in and out. As you continue to watch your breath, it is slowing down, and your mind has become calm. As your heart becomes quiet and your mind becomes still, a mysterious door appears before you. You walk through the door and enter into a new world—a portal from the physical world to the spiritual world. You are in a magical room where time seems slow. The walls are made of luminous white light. There is unique spiritual energy here; this energy is inviting you to let go of all your old habitual ways of thinking. Gently but firmly, you let go of all the old thoughts that are running through your mind. You become totally present in the moment and enter into a mystical quiet.

As you enter into this serenity, another mysterious door appears before you. You are drawn to enter into another chamber. It is filled with golden orange light. Above you, there is a white pulsating point of light. There are soft white concentric circles of white light emanating from this exquisite star. The luminous light is alive; there is a beauty and depth to it that is making you feel very tranquil and welcomed. Like a needle drawn to a magnet you become one with the star. Cascades of luminous white light are pouring over you.

With each cascade, your worries go away, the feeling of striving leaves you and your breath becomes very slow. The feeling of needing to be anything for anyone goes away, and you become pure and simple. As the light washes over you, you move more and more deeply into silence.

Being close to this luminous star feels as if you have touched eternity. It feels as if you've been here forever and known this star forever. You feel timeless and free. Free from the past and free to be who you were born to be—a beautiful self-sovereign soul.

As a cascade of light from the Source washes over you, a recognition stirs deep within you. A realization that you are a sovereign with extraordinary spiritual powers and a vast fortune of virtue. You have complete mastery. The instant you need a virtue, you command it, and it becomes present as a minister would for his king. These special attributes are bringing a feeling of peace, purity, and prosperity to you in this moment. Take a few more moments and absorb this energy.

When you are ready, slowly come back to the room you are sitting in. You come back with a longing for the freedom you once knew and the power you once had. You also come back with insights. You understand that nurturing stillness over a long period of time and taking power from the Source brings you in touch with your self-sovereignty and access to your vast fortune.

Om Shanti – I am Peace.

OH MY GOODNESS! IT WORKS!

Thank you for taking your valuable time to read this book. My goal was to share with you a global picture of essential virtues and why you should cultivate them. Because all virtues come from the same place, the pure soul, your practice of one virtue strengthens your soul and so enables you to advance toward all the other virtues. Purity and virtue are the intrinsic nature of the soul. Hence, as you cultivate virtue, you progress in your self-realization.

As you practice the principles of this book, you will notice that goodness grows in you like a multifaceted diamond. All the virtues are but facets of a single most valuable diamond – you, the pure soul. And your pure self is the source of happiness and wisdom. As souls, we are by nature consciousness, and in our pure state, that consciousness is transparent like crystalline water. So, as you practice the virtues presented in this book, you purify your consciousness, and so you see everything as it really is. With that clear vision, you achieve ultimate happiness.

To achieve authentic happiness and lasting joy, you must engage your virtues in practical action. Just by the act of reflecting on a virtue, you begin to cultivate that virtue. Deep reflection brings virtue back into your life. Your reflection on one virtue feeds the other virtues. And, as you advance in one virtue, it becomes easier for you to cultivate the others. Therefore, you have the power to achieve a great life, simply by putting the tools in this book to good use.

If you've read this book, you are already well on your way to a deeply satisfying life. I encourage you to keep referring to the book again and again. As I mentioned in the beginning, every morning, open the book to any page, pick the virtue listed on that page, and tell yourself, "This is the virtue I will practice today." The universe of virtues works in magical ways. I've noticed that the virtue you need that day will appear to you. You will give your day an added resource to make it truly enjoyable. You should also use this book when you have to make an important decision or when you are embarking on a new project. Again, open the book to a random page and make that virtue your north star to guide that project or situation. You will notice a significant shift in the way you approach life. Virtue fills a void in us that cannot be filled with any number of physical toys.

Virtue also addresses the mind-body connection. It not only gives you a satisfying life, but it also helps the body to heal. Virtue transforms every aspect of our life and every person we meet. It extends from our self to our relationships, and ultimately to the environment and our entire planet. Virtue will heal our bodies, our minds, our relationships, and our troubled world. More than ever, our planet needs good people. Cultivate your natural goodness, and just by living a virtuous life, you will do more for yourself and our planet that you can now imagine. This book is your companion and friend on that journey.

AFTERWORD

Brahma Baba, the founder of the Brahma Kumaris, was the target of several assassination attempts because in the ultra-conservative India of the 1930s, he advocated that women be spiritual leaders and take control of their lives. The Sindhi community, of which Brahma Baba and all his female adherents were members, violently opposed this. On one occasion several of the women's fathers, brothers, and husbands hired a man to kill Baba.

The hired assassin came to the small campus where Brahma Baba and many of his followers were living. Baba was in the courtyard, and he sensed that this man did not have the best of intentions. So, he immediately went into a deep state of meditation and remembrance of the Supreme Soul.

At that moment, several people in the campus who were engaged in various chores such as washing clothes, cooking, cleaning or gardening, felt that they must go to Baba. This small group dropped whatever they were doing and went to look for Brahma Baba. They quickly came and surrounded Baba.

That man saw these people surround Brahma Baba and he left. Baba asked one of the sisters to get toli (a sacred sweet prepared in remembrance of the Supreme). He gave toli to everyone who surrounded him, and while still in deep meditation, the only statement Baba made was, "Virtue is our only protection."

The assassin came the next day to ask Brahma Baba for forgiveness. The man said that all he saw when he looked at Baba was light and he could not carry out the terrible deed that he came to do. Brahma Baba gave the man toli and sent him away.

Later on, Brahma Baba said that everyone who had a particular virtue felt a pull from the Supreme Soul to come and surround Baba. His own virtues protected him by drawing to him other virtuous people.

I heard this story from a Dadi (a senior spiritual sister) who was actually there on the campus at that time. This story had a powerful impact on me. For the first few years of my spiritual practice, I used to reflect on this story almost daily and wonder, what is threatening me right now? If you think about it, we are assaulted by our own doubts, insecurities, material hankerings, envy, jealousy, lust, greed, anger etc. I used to tell myself, "If I give in to my lower instincts, they will destroy me." And, "If I'm sincere and connect to the Source, then the Supreme will send me protectors in the form of remembrance, a higher understanding, will power, clarity, courage etc.

This book came into being as a result of my daily musings on the power of virtue. I hope you enjoyed reading it as much as I enjoyed writing it. Actually, more than simply enjoying the writing process, I took immense benefit from reflecting on the contents as I prepared them for you. It took me to a higher plane of consciousness each and every single time I sat with it. In my personal life, this book has already done its job!

ACKNOWLEDGEMENTS

This book came into being with the help and inspiration of so many. May the blessings I received from them return to them a hundredfold.

I offer my special thanks to the following:

Shukriya **BapDada** for teaching me to be comfortable in my own skin, to own every moment, and to find a home in your heart.

My spiritual elders — **Dadi Janki,** and **Sisters Mohini and Waddy**. Your thoughts are wings that lift souls into the light of their own virtues. My heartfelt thanks for lighting my path and encouraging me.

My family — **Amma, Nana, Malini**, and **Shilpa** for their constant, unconditional love, expressed in so many practical ways. Thank you for always being there. I feel blessed to belong to you.

Dr. Howard Resnick (aka Acharyadeva) — You serve with a pure heart. Thank you for your friendship and tireless dedication to editing this book.

Judy Johnson and team - There is a special sweetness in your valuable words. Thank you for helping edit this book.

Dr. Leddy Hammock — With God as your companion, you create such love within your heart that you are able to silently give it to everyone you meet. Thank you for doing the copy edits, though I asked you at the last minute.

Helen Blaaker, Ritu Gopalan, and **Martha Marquez** — You are always in God's hands. And so, there are only bright skies ahead of you. Thank you for taking on the task of editing and posting the audio meditations of this book.

Judi Rich — In your smile and in your actions, you radiate virtue. Thank you for making the book covers and all between the covers look so beautiful.

Karen Perusse — Your steady peaceful presence in our community helped me to focus on this book.

The Brahma Kumaris Tampa family and all my friends. You and I understand that these are precious days. You possess the treasure of God and hence your lives are successful. Thank you for your love and company.